Kingdom MENTALITY

DR. OSCAR PELAEZ

Dr. Oscar Pelaez

This book is written to provide information and motivation to readers. Its purpose is not to render any type of psychological, legal, or professional advice of any kind. The content is the sole opinion and expression of the author, and not necessarily that of the publisher.

Copyright © 2021 by Dr. Oscar Pelaez.

All rights reserved. No part of this book may be reproduced, transmitted, or distributed in any form by any means, including, but not limited to, recording, photocopying, or taking screenshots of parts of the book, without prior written permission from the author or the publisher. Brief quotations for noncommercial purposes, such as book reviews, permitted by Fair Use of the U.S. Copyright Law, are allowed without written permissions, as long as such quotations do not cause damage to the book's commercial value. For permissions, write to the publisher, whose address is stated below.

Printed in the United States of America.

ISBN   978-1-955363-14-3   (Paperback)
ISBN   978-1-955363-15-0   (Digital)

Lettra Press books may be ordered through booksellers or by contacting:

Lettra Press LLC
30 N Gould St. Suite 4753
Sheridan, WY 82801
1 307-200-3414 | info@lettrapress.com
www.lettrapress.com

TABLE OF CONTENTS

Introduction v

Chapter 1   Recovering the King's Mind 1

Chapter 2   The Appearance of God 6

Chapter 3   The Crown of Power 9

Chapter 4   God Knows you by Your Thoughts. 12

Chapter 5   The King and Priest's Ministry 16

Chapter 6   Faith is a Condition to Have a Relationship with God......................23

Chapter 7   The Mentality of Determination 29

Chapter 8   The Breakthrough of the Kingdoms 33

Chapter 9   Destroy Deceitfulness by Obedience 41

Chapter 10   "Recover your Territory." 46

Prayer of Salvation 58

About the Book 59

INTRODUCTION

THREE YEARS OF WORK DRAFTING this book were the price paid to bring something good to the world's nations. Since the words written in this book more than a theory are a spiritual experience of intimacy with God, every place I can share the word of God, there is always a manifestation of His presence. People have called me from many places, expressing to have an encounter with God while reading the words in this book. God has used the manuscript to restore marriages, restore the first love for the things of the Lord on multitudes, and restore faith in the promises of the Lord through the Scriptures because the divine purpose that He still has with your life is not over, but it is yet to come!

God Bless you,
The Author

Prophecy Given to Dr. Oscar Pelaez Apostle & Prophet.
In the Year 2014

These are the words of the Lord Almighty: Beginning the Month of September of 2018, I will open the gates of financial favor, and I will bless my people from the North to the south, from East to West. I will begin from Israel, then the United States, and last to my people on the rest of the world's nations. I will pour out my Spirit upon my people with beautiful garments, and financial favor says the Lord before the angel sounds a trumpet of judgment to begin upon the earth. Now it is time to believe and never look back, and everything you have supposed for will come to pass. I will use the leader in the white house, the president, to restore everything that the enemy has been stealing from my people, says the Lord Almighty!

CHAPTER ONE

RECOVERING THE KING'S MIND

"Then the LORD God formed a man from the dust of the
ground and breathed into his nostrils the breath of life, and
the man became a living being."
Gen. 2:7 (NIV)

The word dust in Hebrew is "Aphar," which means:

- The smallest particles of the ground
- The driest particles of the ground
- The smallest ashes from the earth
- Dry or lose ground.

THE WORD GROUND MEANS IN Hebrew "Land, territory or country." When we put the above verse of Genesis 2:7 into the real root of the Hebrew, it becomes interpreted like this:

God created the man, made him a sensitive living soul in the spiritual realm, and understood that he carries within himself the land, territory, country, or ground that belongs to him from the very beginning. So, I Understand, the moment in which the sole of my feet touches the same ground that it is within us, whatever we ask for, it will come to pass! I hope you have ears to hear what the Spirit is revealing to you right now.

The man was created from the most sensitive ground particles of the earth, so he should be more Spirit than flesh. The Bible never says that Adam was made from the dirt ground; the animals were created from the dirt ground; the Bible says that man was created from the surface "Aphar-dust" of the earth. Let me help you understand quickly; God Created him, but to allow him to be seen in the Garden, God had to use some particles from the dust "Aphar" to enable him to be placed in the Garden with all the authority as the image of God!

Are you listening to what I am saying?

Let us see what the Hebrew Aramaic dictionary says about the word image. The word "image" means:

"Tselem," which means "the same appearance." God took the appearance of a man to enter the earthly atmosphere and still be God.

Just a little thought, God took the appearance of man to live on earth as a man, and men will take the divine appearance of God during the rapture to be in heaven as "Elohim," or small God. We have the same appearance of God on the earth, on the ground level. Let me affirm your faith by supporting this illumination with the Scriptures of the word of God: The Bible says on Genesis 32:26, *"Then the man said, "Let me go, for it is daybreak." But Jacob replied, "I will not let you go unless you bless me."* You see in this passage that Jacob struggled with God as a man to receive his blessing, which means that Jacob and "Tselem" = The God of human appearance was withheld from Jacob until He blessed him.

The words "in our likeness" in Hebrew is written "Demuwth," which means similitude, like, equal, manner, fashion. We can easily understand by those definitions that we are to have the same personality as God. In other words, you and I received identity, personality, fatherhood, and character by the likeness of God. When we say in this title, "recovering the king's mind," we need to talk about mentality, and this is the question, what is kingdom mentality? Let me give you different concepts for you to understand better. Kingdom mentality means changing the perception of how we see things. The way we perceive things is the way our understanding works things out in the natural. You can see problems with your discouraged emotional mentality, but God can see opportunities for training you to your next level of faith. Are you listening to what I am saying?

Let me give you one example: *2 Kings 6: 11-19 "This enraged the King of Aram. He summoned his officers and demanded of them, "Tell me! Which of us is on the side of the King of Israel?" "None of us, my lord the king," said one of his officers, "but*

Elisha, the prophet who is in Israel, tells the king of

Israel the very words you speak in your bedroom." "Go, find out where he is," the King ordered, "so I can send men and capture him." The report came back: "He is in Dothan." Then he sent horses and chariots and a strong force there. They went by night and surrounded the city. When the servant of the man of God got up and went out early the following day, an army with horses and chariots had surrounded the city."

Oh no! My lord! What shall we do?" the servant asked. "Don't be afraid," the prophet answered. "Those who are with us are more than those who are with them." And Elisha prayed, "Open his eyes, LORD, so that he may see." Then the LORD opened the servant's eyes, and he looked and saw the hills full of horses and chariots of fire all around Elisha. As the enemy came down toward him, Elisha prayed to the LORD, "Strike this army with blindness." So, he struck them with blindness, as Elisha had asked. Elisha told them, "This is not the road, and this is not the city. Follow me, and I will lead you to the man you are looking for." And he led them to Samaria.

In other words, no matter how your present situation looks today or how much the enemy trapped you on the road. Still, God has horses and chariots around you to protect you and show you the way out; the only thing He needs from you is to open your spiritual eyes so you can perceive and see from another dimension, the dimension of the kingdom of God. Are you with me?

Do not ever say anymore you cannot do it, do not ever say again, God has forgotten about me. Do not ever say" I am alone," because everything you need to get out from where you are to the other side of the problem is within you. The only thing you need is to have the correct perception of the world around you. The moment you learn how the King of the kingdom sees things, you would be able to see challenges and no difficulties, which is because of your new perception. In other words, developing a new perception of the world around us will allow us to demonstrate His power!

It says in the Scriptures: *"The eyes of your understanding being enlightened; that ye may know what the hope of his calling is, and what the riches of the glory of his inheritance in the saints." Eph. 1:18 (NKJV)*

Kingdom mentality in the spiritual means is how our faith is moving in the dimension that the kingdom of God moves to interact with men, respond to men's petitions with power, and manifest his promises. That way of thinking makes you understand your position on earth, knowing that God has given you an authority on the top of any principality of darkness to use it and not to quit the battle. It says in the Scriptures: *"Which he wrought in Christ when he raised him from the dead and set him at his right hand in the heavenly places, far above all principality, and power, and might, and dominion, and every name that is named, not only in this world but also in that which is to come; and hath put all things under his feet and gave him to be the head over all things to the church, which is his body, the fullness of him that fill all in all." Eph. 1:20-23 (New King James Version)*

Jesus' commission on earth was full of opposition and difficulties, but He never quit; that is why He is at the right hand of the father. Elisha was exposed to be terrified when the perception of his servant was fearfully and not faithfully, but he chose to believe in God, the one that is never late! He is always on time to respond to those that understand how the principles of the kingdom work. Glory to God! Kingdom mentality also must be with declaring words of faith with a positive attitude. For example: In verse 18, look what the prophet said," *As the enemy came down toward him, Elisha prayed to the LORD, "Strike this army with blindness." So, he struck them with blindness, as Elisha had asked.* Belief is one thing but exercising your authority is another thing. You can believe that God will get you out of trouble, but you need to open your mouth and declare what you want to happen, and you will see God move on your behalf. Stop complaining that

you did not get that job or that contract or that promotion if you did everything right. Sometimes the root of the problem is in the spiritual realm, and you need to begin to learn how to open your eyes as Elisha did and see from God's perspective.

Hallelujah!

Kingdom mentality is to understand the perfect will of God and obey it. You may ask, "What should I do?" Let me tell you what works for me until I recover everything that the enemy had stolen from me in certain areas of my life, exercise warfare. It says in the word of God in the book of *Judges*

Chapter 3 verses 1-4, "These are the nations the LORD left to test all those Israelites who had not experienced any of the wars in Canaan. (he did this only to teach warfare to the descendants of the Israelites who had not had previous battle experience): the five rulers of the Philistines, all the Canaanites, the Sidonians, and the Hivites living in the Lebanon mountains from Mount Baal Hermon to Lebo Hamath. They were left to test the Israelites to see whether they would obey the LORD's commands, which he had given their ancestors through Moses. It is written in the Hebrew dictionary "Milchamah," *which means warfare. The word "warfare" means to fight, to battle. The same term applies to either spiritual or natural warfare. Look at what the verse says, to teach warfare to the descendants of the Israelites who had no previous battle experience. If right now you know, you are not in disobedience, you are not in sin, you are giving your tithes and offerings and congregate in church regularly, but problems keep coming from every angle. Let me tell you, dear brother and sister, God is training you to learn how to do warfare!*

One of the things that people ignore is that in every battle against every group, there was a principality that they had to overcome. For example, the word Philistines: "Pĕlishtiy" means a ruler. It also means an intimidator. The word Canaanites: "Kĕna'aniy" means a negotiator. The word Sidonians: "Tsiydoniy" means a hunter. The word Hivites:

Chivviy" means a villager, the ones that have eyes to recognize a good land and possess. God chooses each specific nation to train you in each area of your life and make you stronger than your enemy so, when the "Philistines" send schemes of fear, your faith will be stronger, and trust your God. When the hunter "Sidonians" come to trap you, the strategies of God, the voice of God, will bring show you the way out. No, you are not listening! When you do business with the "Canaanites," the wisdom of God will shine within you, so you do not make bad investments. Glory to God!

We need to do warfare, so these nations do not take upon your villages, your territory, or your business. From today on, practice fighting in the Spirit by making the proper declarations. Do it at least once a week but be sensitive when God prompts you to do it no matter what day or time because the prayer of the righteous has power. Warfare is more than a simple prayer; it is more than just praying within your mind; warfare is crying out after God declares what you believe and wants them to happen.

Every time you do a little bit of warfare, begin to make positive confessions about your destiny, finances, family, ministry, or whatever you believe; follow the river of the Holy Spirit because whatever you declare on earth, it will happen on the heavens. I like to say: I am the head and not the tail, I lend too many and never ask to borrow, I have the mentality to be a ruler, to be an administrator, to be a governor by exercising the authority from earth to heaven. I declare that He created me like a king to give me a kingdom that will manifest heaven on earth by executing the right kingdom mentality.

Dear brother, I pray that the mind of the King that Jesus returned to you through the cross and the power of his resurrection *wake up your Spirit!* You are not what the enemy says you are! You are what God says you are, and that is your anchor to hold on. Remember, you are crown with Jesus at the right hand of the father. Please put this teaching into practice, and you will see good results in your life. You will recover the mind of the King, especially if you are passing through the valley of the shadow of death because it is never too late to believe and to begin to exercise authority one more time. Amen.

God Bless you!

CHAPTER TWO
THE APPEARANCE OF GOD

"Anyone who has seen me has seen the Father." John 14:9

I WANT TO BEGIN BY SAYING that the devil is an expert on evil schemes who knows how to destroy our image of who we are in Christ. You can be an ordained minister or just a regular church-going Christian; he sends his arrows and schemes to both. There are arrows of fear and discouragement continually bombarding our minds, and if we do not renew our mind always with the Word of God, we will begin to doubt our authority in Christ and end up losing most of the battles in our daily walk.

Many people come to me asking for counseling because they feel like they are under constant attack. They love God; they are faithful in their tithes and offerings; they are not walking in sin. They wonder what they are doing wrong. When I pray to God, the answer I received is that they are not doing anything wrong. It is just religious opposition. The devil had stolen the "Yatsar's of heaven" *given to man when he was formed from the beginning.*

"And the Lord God formed man of the dust of the ground and breathed into his nostrils the breath of life; man became a living soul' Genesis 2:7. Let us analyze the word "formed" from the above verse: The term "form" means in Hebrew "Yatsar," which means to be framed, to be preordained, and to be designed. *In simple words, "Yatsar" means to have the same appearance of God in the spirit realm.* Jesus walked on earth into the "Yatsar" of God when he said in *John 14:9, "Anyone who has seen me has seen the Father."* Jesus understood that the image of his father would shine through him everywhere he went by the power of activating the "Yatsar."

Demons move in the spiritual realm, and if they can recognize Jesus in your countenance, they will back down. For example, in the book of *Acts 16:17, a woman that had a spirit of divination showed up to the apostle's Paul and Barnabas. The same followed Paul and us, and cried, saying, these men are the servants of the highest God, which show unto us the way of salvation."*

The bible says that it came to pass when they were praying. They were not doing anything else at the time.

They were at the house of this humble woman, and the spirit of divination showed up and recognized the image of the all-powerful God in the mortal bodies of the apostles.

Let us be practical and apply a little bit of this to our daily lives. When God formed the man, the "Yatsar" was given to him as a privilege to be like God. Every time man gets into the spirit realm, whether by prayer or by fasting to do spiritual warfare, the kingdom of darkness is subdued under his feet because "the Yatsar" spiritual realm comes down

and reactivates his authority, covering him with the cloud of God's presence.

You and I have the right to keep those privileges activated every day to control better what is happening in our lives. If you do so, the enemy cannot touch you anymore, neither your health nor your finances. And every evil plan against you shall be destroyed, in the name of Jesus! You may ask me why? Because demons tremble before the presence of God, and when you show up, they do not see you, they see the image, the frame of God the "Yatsar" on you, and they will flee from your presence as they did with Jesus. Glory to God!

Let me give you some biblical support to help you understand once and for all how the "Yatsar" will work for your life. *Mark 9:2-4" Now after six days Jesus took Peter, James, and John, and led them up on a high mountain apart by themselves; and He was transfigured before them. His clothes became shining, exceedingly white, like snow, such as no launderer on earth can whiten them. And Elijah appeared to them with Moses, and they were talking with Jesus.*

One perfect example of the "Yatsar" was this as a human person, like you and me. Jesus on earth must walk like a human, but He always shows us how spiritual spheres can be activated. *Exodus 33:18-23" And he said, "Please, show me Your glory." Then He said, "I will make all My goodness pass before you, and I will proclaim the name of the LORD before you. I will be gracious to whom I will be gracious, and I will have compassion on whom I will have compassion. But He said, "You cannot see My face; for no man shall see Me, and live. And the LORD said, "Here is a place by Me, and you shall stand on the rock. "So, it shall be, while My glory passes by, that I will put you in the cleft of the rock and will cover you with My hand while I pass by. Then I will take away My hand, and you shall see My back, but*

My face shall not be seen."

Moses' job was only to chase after God's presence, to pray to God, and do warfare every day for God's people and His Glory will bless him. Remember, every one of the five thousand promises in the bible will be fulfilled in our lives ONLY if we do the necessary daily warfare. Otherwise, things become retained in the second heaven. God only needs to see us doing His will by praying in faith and confessing the promises of God, and He will bring them to pass.

Dear brother or sister, it is time to shake off the dust, darkness, and negativity out of our minds. Instead, we must retake what belongs to us. It is time to change the opinion that you have about yourself. It is time to forget about the things that happened in the past and press on for new beginnings. Remember, whether good or bad, it is already in the past; stop living from the successful things of yesterday, today it is a new day, full of opportunities to conquer in the name of Jesus! Never forget, God wants you to see yourself again with the image that He created you in the Garden of Adam and Eve because the only opinion that should matter for you is the opinion of God. He loves you just the way you are, and He will always see you as a finished product. He will still see you like the person of God that has reached the level of holiness, faith, and prosperity that He declared upon you the day he formed you.

I believe, when God is about to take his people into a new season, He will always work from the inside out and never from the outside in. Today, if we connect with the Holy Spirit by praying and fasting, it will heal every wound from the past that is affecting our present. It is time that people see Jesus through us. As Jesus said, *"Anyone who has seen me has seen the Father."*

God Bless you!

CHAPTER THREE
THE CROWN OF POWER

"And the soldiers twisted a crown of thorns and put *it* on His head,
and they put on Him a purple robe. Then they said, "Hail, King of the Jews!"
And they struck Him with their hands."
John 19:2-3

MANY PEOPLE NEED TO SEE the spilling of blood from Jesus' head through the eyes of God the Father. He needed to spill blood from his head for us to receive the renewal of our minds.

Jesus said in Mat. *26:42, 'Again, a second time, He went away and prayed, saying, "O My Father, if this cup cannot pass away from Me unless I drink it, your will be done."*

He said those words when He was at the hill of Gethsemane. A cup is used to share joy or success, not the incomparable pain and sorrow that He suffered to seal the victory for all humankind. When a person does not understand that revelation, that sometimes grief and pain must first be felt before the joy of success; most of all, that person is not ready for the next level of breakthrough. Behind every "Crown of Glory," there is a battle that first must be won in the way we think every single day. "As a man thinks in his heart, so is he." Jesus came to his people expecting them to have a godlier mentality because they were a chosen generation of God. They were a generation that knew the God of Abraham, Isaac, and Jacob. But it was not as He expected; instead, he found that they had the spirit of religiosity. That is the spirit that the devil used to kill Jesus. That spirit was in the way they thought.

The scriptures say in the book of **Romans 12:2,** *"and be not conformed to this world, but the renewing of your mind transforms ye."* Jesus came to His people, but his people did not receive Him because they did not belong to Him" Why? Because their minds were never renewed! An account that is not replaced is like a car in need of a tune-up. What Jesus was saying is that if their minds were not open to something new, then they will never have the understanding to recognize the Son of the Living God.

The power of the blood being shed from his head is the one thing that opened the door for us to have a "new kingdom mentality." If you study the scriptures, you will see that before our souls were redeemed from eternal condemnation, Jesus restored the way we think with the crown of Glory! Why? Because if He had not done that, even though He went to the cross and died for all humanity, we might not have recognized him as the Son of God. We may have believed he was just another prophet, along with many others in the history of Judah, who died for his beliefs. Hallelujah!

I was once in the library of a Jewish temple, and I asked one of the deacons," What do they think about Jesus?" And they answered," We believe in Jesus.

Still, we do not recognize Him as a Savior. We acknowledge Him as a well-respected prophet, just like Abraham, Isaac, and Jacob, and the other prophets of the house of Israel." You can see they worship God that their minds are not renewed. They may study the scriptures, but without renewing their minds, there will be no changes to the way they see salvation. Unless the atonement of the lamb is recognized, nothing new will happen in our lives. There is so much power in the blood of Jesus, and when that power is accepted, the blood that Jesus shed from his head will change the way we use ours!

I want to close the chapter with another situation that happened to me concerning the redeeming of our minds. I went another day to a Jewish temple, and they were celebrating the feast of the Yom Kippur. One memorable dinner to celebrate the beginning of the new year according to the Jewish calendar.

Before I arrived, I prayed to the Holy Spirit. I said,

"Holy Spirit, I want to feel the God of Isaiah, Abraham, and Moses when I am among your chosen people, the people that you love most of all!" Then I went into the temple and received the Yamaka upon my head. They explained that since it was my first time, I must sit in a particular room with other new visitors, but I would be able to see the service in its entirety and participate as I feel led. I did just that. I read the same scriptures that they read, and I bowed down before the God of Moses, Abraham, and Jacob. After doing all of that with faith and reverence, I did not feel a thing. I inquired of God, "God, I am here among your chosen people; I asked for your perfect touch that I might feel what they feel? Two hours have passed, and I do not feel anything! Where are you?" He answered, "Where are you?" and I said," right among your chosen people worshipping you. "He responded to me, "Son, my mercy is here, but my presence is not!" I asked Him, why You are not in here amid your chosen people? He answered," *BECAUSE MY PRESENCE CANNOT BE IN ANY PLACE THAT THE BLOOD OF MY SON IS NOT RECOGNIZED."* That is why it is essential for you, dear reader, to understand that there may be a *"New World Order" that is coming, but at the same time, there is a New Kingdom Mentality* that God wants His people to embrace where everything begins and ends with the blood of Christ that was shed for us! Some may laugh at this principle just like the Romans soldiers did, but let me tell you, those soldiers that witnessed the power of His resurrection were no longer laughing but trembling with fear. I encourage you to make this declaration every morning. "I have the mind of Christ. I cover all my thoughts under the blood of Jesus." You will soon see that the enemy cannot win the battle in your daily life because you are the one who will determine how you want your day to be.

God Bless You!

CHAPTER FOUR

GOD KNOWS YOU BY YOUR THOUGHTS.

"For my thoughts are not your thoughts,
neither are your ways my ways."
Isaiah. 55:8

BEFORE GOD SAW THE LIGHT and green pastures, He saw darkness. When we talk about the Mentality of our creator, what it means is that even if you are in a financial mess, or you are having a health problem, and you are in terrible pain, you are going through a divorce. God is still in control of your life if you allow Him to move on your behalf.

God is always looking for situations that are impossible for men to resolve, so He can step up and be God! I have come to tell you that God has not been delaying bringing an answer to your prayers. The problem is that your mind will not believe that He can do it one more time.

When our minds stop believing that He is the Almighty, that He can do and moves in the supernatural, then we have a problem! Remember, there are no problems in the Mentality of God, only challenges. The only problem for God is when people stop believing and forget that the supernatural is the very atmosphere of God. Are you listen to what I am saying?

I can tell you that when you stop focusing on your mess and begin to shift your focus to God, the "Mentality of your Creator" will come back to you. How? By the power of the Holy Spirit! He is even more eager than you are to help you recover the level of Mentality that His chosen people should have. When you let Him turn your bitterness into sweetness, then negativity will have no place in your life. Glory to God!

Let me tell you why God allowed you to go through those times of testing in the wilderness. He wanted you to develop a new mind. Remember, God will exalt those humble, and He will bring down those who have a high opinion of themselves.

The Bible says in the book of Psalms 139:23," Search me, oh God, and know my heart; test me and know my anxious thoughts." He wants you to know why you have not received the things that you are asking? It is for a reason. He is God, and the plans He has for you are right, and His blessings are to bless you and not destroy you. You never know how many times He has passed by your thoughts to see if you were ready for a blessing, but you were not. Let me tell you this; do not give up! He who begins a good work in you will perform it until the day of the Lord.

Sometimes our sorrow becomes a platform for God to establish in us a new way of thinking from the inside out, a new kingdom mentality so He can bring us to the other side of the river whether it is in our ministry, our finances, our health, or our marriage. The Act of redemption did not begin with Jesus; it started with God's Father, who made the plan of redemption for humankind. The Bible says that Jesus is our Redeemer, which means the one who performed or accomplished God's goal of redemption.

When studying the book of Genesis, we see that Adam and Eve did not have a clue that the voice of God was the law of the Garden. The first law came from the voice of God. He said that you would not eat from the tree of knowledge, which means to guard your mind.

The second law came from God through Moses, and it was "The Ten Commandments." Jesus was crowned with that crown of sorrow because the first thing that man lost in the Garden was his Mentality, so the blood needed to be shed first from the head of Jesus, so the rest of the body of Christ will recover a freedom mentality. One thing that you need to know is that Satan noticed that Adam and Eve ignored the fact that the law of the Garden was the voice of God. I am sure God established the same rule in heaven, "His Voice," and the angels that violated were rebuked from heaven.

That is the same spiritual law that Moses violated when he lost the privilege to enter the promised land. The voice of God is a law. God told Moses to speak to the rock, and instead, he struck the rock twice. *Num. 20:8-12 (NKJV)*

"Take the staff, and you and your brother Aaron gather the assembly together. Speak to that rock before their eyes, and it will pour out its water. You will bring water out of the rock for the community so they and their livestock can drink. So, Moses took the staff from the LORD's presence, just as he commanded him. He and Aaron gathered the assembly together in front of the rock, and Moses said to them, "Listen, you rebel, must we bring you water out of this rock. "Then Moses raised his arm and struck the rock twice with his staff. Water gushed out, and the community and their livestock drank. But the LORD said to Moses and Aaron,

"Because you did not trust in me enough to honor me as holy in the sight of the Israelites, you will not bring this community into the land I give them." Behind every crown of Glory, there is a crown of sorrow. There was a prophetic line of understanding when Jesus was crowned with the crown of thorns; powerful things happened due to this action. When He received the crown of sorrow and blood was spilled out of his head, he was redeeming the thinking of all humankind.; all of that includes the way we think, the way we perceive things, and the way we believe matters. I hope you understand the power of this. Those that recognized his blood were renewed in their minds immediately.

Have you ever questioned why Jesus did not appear after his resurrection first to his right hand, Peter, or to the rest of his staff (disciples) before anybody else?

What I believe is the answer. Peter and his disciples did not see the crown of redemption; they saw the crown of crucifixion. Are you listening? They saw one more prophet on the cross that God used on behalf of Israel, and until the power of the blood touched their minds, nothing was renewed in their mentalities. Mary Magdalene was the last one at the cross, which means she was touch first by the power of the resurrection. According to their NEW MENTALITY, Jesus appeared to people after his resurrection; Mary Magdalene was the first person to see him because there is power in the blood of Jesus. That is why it is so important to have the Holy Communion in our congregations; believe me; there is more power in those elements than you realize! Jesus did not show himself after the resurrection until the people's minds were renewed! *Why is this so important? Because in the new covenant, everything is about faith, and that faith is the one thing that will help you understand how the kingdom works.*

Developing the Mentality of The King takes time and practice, and it can only happen through a relationship with the Holy Spirit.

The body of Christ is full of many kings by appearance, but within their minds are far away from acting like one.

I urge you to connect to the promises of the Word of God that are in this book. I declare that every time you read them, your confidence will begin to spark up, and your mind will begin to shine and be renewed in the name of Jesus Christ. I declare that you are essential and precious before the eyes of God and everything that you have lost in every area of your life; God will return seventy times seven plus interest into your hands! I declare that the Mentality of the king that God has given you is rising within your spirit and your soul because He created you to be the head and not the tail.

God created man from the very beginning with the same Mentality as His, "the mentality of a king." The Bible says in the book of *Genesis 1:27 So, God created man in his image, in God, He created him; male and female he created them.*

New Kingdom Mentality is an incredibly special impartation that The Holy Spirit reveals about *how the kingdom works.* It is the clear understanding of who we are in Christ and for what purpose we were created? The people of God have missed an ingredient between being saved and reaching their destiny. "Repossess a Godly mentality" *As I have said many times, you can read a book and ignore the name of the author. People read the Bible and do not have a relationship with the author of the Bible.*

I believe this book is the perfect tool to encourage and edify the body of Christ in these turbulent times, as well as challenge the faith of those who love the Lord and have the desire to serve him as vessels of his Glory.

I want you to see by faith that this book is not in your hands by accident; it *is coming to you now at the right time in the perfect seaso*n. I believe God was waiting for you to get tired of your usual way of doing things, which is usually a result of religiosity. *Remember that God works in mysterious ways. The verse of Isa55:8 says, "for my thoughts are not your thoughts, neither are your ways my ways."* Let God show and reveal to you whatever His will is; let Him be as close to us as we are close to Jesus by the power of his blood. Amen.

God Bless you!

CHAPTER FIVE

THE KING AND PRIEST'S MINISTRY

"And has made us kings and priests to His God and
Father, to Him be glory and dominion forever and ever."
Rev1:6

THE WRONG INTERPRETATION ABOUT THE Ministry of the Priest and Kings has locked the church's power in many areas, especially finances.

The Bible says in the book of *Hosea 4:6,* *"my people are destroyed from lack of knowledge. "Because you have rejected knowledge, I also reject you as my priests; because you have ignored the law of your God, I also will forget your children.*

Many people do not realize that the early apostolic church believed that He would return soon after his resurrection. That was one of the main reasons nobody focused or worried too much about prosperity in the early church. Because of this lack of financial vision, many were unable to effectively preach the gospel of Jesus due to lack of finances.

Today, monetary funds are one of the biggest challenges that churches used to struggle with. The Use of perception of this weakness, satanic churches have been known to send wealthy people to infiltrate a Christian church as a tactic to destroy them. One tactic is the influence on the pastor and leadership through making unique offerings. I know of a few cases in which wealthy women send by satanic cults purchased the grace of the pastors or leaders to gain influence in the church and then used that influence to create division and destroy the unity of the flock. Those are foreshadowed of how the Antichrist will gain power when seated as a

European Global Common Market director. Presidents of many nations will be deceived by how much money he has, how much influence, how many connections, and they will judge him by his outside appearance.

Be careful!

The lack of finances in many churches has created an image of poverty and necessity in people's minds.

For this reason, many people do not want to be Christian and assemble in a local church. I know of very wealthy people in the business that left their own companies to serve the Lord when, that was not what God was calling them to do. He was trying to add the Ministry of the "Priest" because they were already "Kings" by the mantle of owning a company. God is a God that adds and multiplies; the devil is the one that subtracts and divides.

Why is all of this happening? It is because of the wrong mentality of the early apostolic church regarding prosperity. Thank God for the people that

God has raised and anointed to teach the kingdom of God regarding finances. They encourage people to plant a seed into the kingdom of God. The word of God says, *"So they rose early in the morning and went out into the Wilderness of Tekoa; and as they went out, Jehoshaphat stood and said, "Hear me, O Judah, and you inhabitants of Jerusalem: belief in the LORD your God, and you shall be established; believe His prophets, and you shall prosper." 2 Ch. 20:20 (NKJV).* If we believe in the words of his prophets, we will be prosperous. So, all prosperity begins in your spirit by some impartation from God or by a prophetic word. When it connects with your faith, then something will start to manifest on the outside.

For example, giving your tithes and offerings without faith, God will bless you for is ineffective. If you do not believe that the promises of God will begin to operate on your behalf to bless you, do not waste your time doing it. You must expect reward, hope, and harvest; you should expect that something good will come out by your act of faith because every move that a king makes with his finances will always bring reward. Glory to God!

It was the same principle with the creation of man. God created him in His image according to His likeness, just at a lower level. The Hebrew word "Elohim" means we are" little gods" that are the same as Him to exercise the system of Heaven on earth. Since we are kings and priests, we should be thinking of ruling, administrate, and govern. That means that within our hearts, we are priests of the living God. It is sort of like, on the one hand, you got into the business mentality, and on the other, you got into the things of the Ministry. That is an excellent example of the" Ministry of King and Priest." It is not religiosity; it is the reality of inheritance and practical mentality. Let me give you an example of a useful king and priest mentality. You can have all the faith in the world, but your car cannot move without gasoline!

Let us go a little deeper. What does the kingdom mean? In Hebrew, the word kingdom means-" Mamlakah," which means dominion, reign, sovereignty, or realm. Also, the root for 'Malakah' is the Hebrew word "Malak," which means king, queen, one that reigns, full of wisdom, king which means supreme authority, one that rules with wisdom, knowledge, and understanding, also means the one who knows how to maintain position and sovereign dominion.

If we interpret these two words, we can see that their meanings are linked to each other. In other words, *there is no king without a kingdom, but there is a kingdom for every king. What God has for you has your name on it, and nobody can steal it out of your hands! Come on and get excited! There are lands, houses, buildings, contracts, sales and better purchases, divine connections, and favor for positions of authority that belong to you and are waiting for those that understand the Ministry that carries the mantle of the king with the heart of the Priest.*

Suppose God made us kings and priests from the very beginning (The Alpha) that is the same thing that He will do in the book of Revelation at the end (The omega). Dear brothers and sisters, he is expecting nothing less from you in the book of Revelation than the kings and priests that He established from the beginning! The devil is a liar, and I declare that everything that belongs to you, he will have to release back into your hands in the name of Jesus!

It is time to take back what belongs to you. The devil has deceived millions of people as he did with the early church concerning finances. It is time to shake the dirt out of your mind and out of your life and rise! You may feel like Jesus did on the cross. He did not look good on the outside, but God was preparing Him to receive position and authority to begin again within the inside. I have come to tell you, siblings, the battle is not over. God has not finished with you yet, the worst is over, and the best is yet to come!

I know that everyone's faith is at a different level, but to put everyone in the same dimension of faith, let me continue with a few more paragraphs before ending this chapter.

As you can see, you need to know how God created you and how He positioned you from the very beginning. He prepared for you a kingdom of inheritance not only up in Heaven but also here on earth. If He is a king, then you are a prince of the high living God; everything that is His is also yours.

Amen. The second thing that I want to tell you is that God is not obligated to bless everything we do. He has only committed to blessing those works that are according to His will. For example, many books have been published, but only a few were released at the right time in the perfect season. I know He will do anything to make sure His purpose for your life will come to fulfillment. For example, before Jesus came to earth in the physical body, history teaches us that there were four hundred and fifty years of silence. No prophets were mentioned until John the Baptist prepared the way of the Lord just before the Lord Jesus began His Ministry.

My point is that no matter how much necessity was upon the earth, God's heart does not move based on needs. He moves in times and seasons by the faith of men on the planet, and He moves for spheres and dimensions up in Heaven. I hope you are listening! The Bible says in *Gal 4:4-5," But when the fullness of the time had come, God sent forth His Son, born from a woman, born under the law. "To redeem those who were under the law, that we might receive the adoption as sons." And because you are sons, God has sent forth the Spirit of His Son into your hearts, crying out, "Abba, Father!"*

He sent His only one song at the right time in the perfect season on earth. Only God knows what was cooking behind the scenes in the kingdom of darkness when He set up the appointed time for the feet of Jesus to touch the earth. Until the man that God created in the spirit touched the ground earth (kingdom), then the power of authority will be delegated. Hallelujah!

When a man does not understand the times and the seasons for his life, he will struggle during his Christian walk, and the results will be *wounded faith*. When your faith is affected, the visions and the dreams for your life are on standby. You love God, you love your family, you go to church, and so on, but concerning Ministry, you try to move forward, but you cannot go anymore because your faith is down. There are thousands of servants of God around the world in the same spot; I have good news to encourage you and teach you how to get back on track and move in the power of the Spirit once again. Never forget that He is a good father that wants all his children to enjoy the seasons of prosperity that come to the earth. The perfect season is just the alignment of your will on earth with God's purpose in Heaven.

The earth moves in seasons, which has to do with time. Heaven moves in dimensions, which has to do with spheres. The spheres are constant; they are the same. That is why the Bible says that "He is a shadow that never changes" or in the book of revelations that He says:" I am the Alpha and the omega "because, in the dimension that He dwells in, time does not exist.

The same Glory he beheld during creation is the same one that He will reveal in Revelation. Hallelujah!'

I want you to keep in mind that no matter how much need was in the earth, God didn't send his son until the right time for the fulfillment of the prophecy." *But when the fullness of the time had come, God sent forth His Son, born from a woman, born under the law.* Therefore, no matter what you went through or are going through, God is still in control of your life just as He was in control of the earth during the four hundred fifty years of silence. The devil may have said to you that God has forgotten about you, but I declare that your mind is free from negativity in the name of Jesus. When you may feel like He is not answering any of your prayers, and He is not speaking to you as before, let me tell you, you are not forgotten! He is observing you all the time, working within your character, and purify your heart about serving the Lord for the right motivation.

Money is the last thing that a person of God should focus on when serving in the Ministry. The Bible says in *3 John 1:2," Beloved, I pray that you may prosper in all things and be in health, just as your soul prospers.*

It is not that he does not want us to prosper and have money; it is the love of money that takes the man's heart in the wrong direction. Are you with me? Another area you need to analyze is your relationship with God and your relationship with your spouse. When God created man, He gave him many things, as I explained in my other chapters; He gave him authority, dominion, makes him a ruler, and on and on but, only when God gave him a woman, the Bible says that He blessed them. *Gen 5:2" He created them male and female and blessed them and called them Mankind in the day they were made."*

The first thing that every man and woman of God needs to ask is, "Why are my finances as they are?

And why is my faith on the floor?

The answer is simple because there has been no balance within your marriage, or if you are single, there has been no balance within your relationship with God. Partial obedience is disobedience. Let your spirit listen to this; the *man was created, already knew the garden, and had a relationship with God and all the animals but, he still was not happy, and he even was not being blessed yet. Only when God gave him a woman, he received his blessing. It is not that if you do not have a wife, you cannot prosper; it is that your wife gives you the balance to exercise authority and administer the blessing that God gave. When God blessed them, it was so much above and beyond their minds that Adam by himself could not handle it.*

Power and authority without balance is chaos, the bride of Jesus was and is the church, and He gave everything for Her. Therefore, God gave everything to Him. My dear friend, I have come to tell you by these words that it is time to recover the authority of your first kingdom, the kingdom of your house. Like King's David, there are many kings out there, he was a hero on the outside, but his first wife, Michal, did not even recognize him as a King. Regardless, how much the tambourine dancers were singing the song

"Saul kill a thousand and David kill ten thousand' David still failed the test because of the wrong perception. Are you listening to what I am saying!

God created man, and in the book of Genesi, He says that "He Blessed them both and he decreed a prophetic word upon them.

Kings and Priest make the right moves in the perfect season.

The perfect season does not mean working more overtime, part-time, and everything that ends in time! An entire season must be with the way you think.

You only need one perfect idea to be put into practice and make the right move to get the breakthrough you are looking to have. Are you listening!

The perfect season is being able to listen to the voice of God in your spirit, something that you know, and you know with the firm conviction that God spoke within your soul, and then you do it. Those are the moments that God uses to restore your faith. He is omnipotent to create within you the capacity to understand His voice.

God never chooses Saul to be the first king of Israel; it was the people that decided to have a visible king.

Saul was never God's plan for his people. Why? Because God knew that he did not have the mentality to be a king.

The Bible says *in Matt 7:16-17, "You will know them by their fruits. Do men gather grapes from thornbushes or figs from thistles?" "Even so, every good tree bears good fruit, but a bad tree bears bad fruit." "A good tree cannot bear bad fruit, nor can a wrong tree bear good fruit.*

Every time King Saul saw David, he always wanted to kill him because a true king carries the anointing within every place they go. There are many kings with garments on the outside on the pulpits placed by man's decisions, but not God's judgments. That is why the kingdom suffers, and his people often do not get the breakthroughs that they should. Now you know the reasons why your second kingdom (church) does not move forward financially.

There is a need for renewal of our minds in the body of Christ because there is so much religiosity that has locked the mentality of millions of kings upon the earth. It is time for David's to rise because they are the only ones that can help others in the body of Christ to recover The New Kingdom Mentality that God has given them.

I am authoring this book to hope that the Holy Spirit touches many leaders worldwide and opens their understanding to receive Revelation about how to keep "recovering the ministry of kings and priests upon the earth."

David was pasturing the sheep that God gave him. God watched him in something that minor, and God began forming the heart of a king, which is the heart of someone that has a fear of God and worships Him, the way he will rule the kingdom. The moment that God put in his father's heart the desire to send him to bring food to his brothers that were getting ready to go to the battle against Goliath *WAS THE APPOINTED PROPHETIC TIME THAT GOD HAD FOR DAVID'S PURPOSE ON EARTH TO SHOW HIM AS THE FUTURE KING.*

DAVID WAS THE ONLY MAN THAT QUALIFIED TO KILL GOLIATH BECAUSE, WHEN THE FAITH OF A MAN IS HEALED AND RESTORED, THE GOLIATHS THAT ARE IN FRONT OF YOU ARE JUST A PIECE OF CAKE IN YOUR HANDS TO KILL. Glory to God!

I want every king and everyone that reads this book to recognize that the perfect seasons are only released into the hands of true kings. When David became the king of Israel, the nation moved in prosperity from Glory to Glory. I urge every pastor, leader, minister, or everyone that wants to give up using the words of this book and begin again, reaching out to God and praying for the renewal of your mind.

We both know that God is a God of order. He always respects the head of the church, but your head, your mentality needs to be renewed so God can release you to bring in the great last harvest of souls that He is preparing for your Ministry before his second coming. I DECLARE THAT GOD WILL USE THE SIMPLES' THINGS AROUND YOU TO BRING YOU TO YOUR DESTINY AND HELP YOU TO RECOVER" THE MINISTRY OF KINGS AND PRIESTS."

I DECLARE THAT JUST LIKE DAVID, BRINGING A SIMPLE LUNCH TO HIS BROTHERS; GOD WILL DO THE SAME THING WITH YOU TO BLESS YOU AND GIVE YOU FAVOR ONCE AGAIN, IN FRONT OF WEALTHY PEOPLE! AMEN.

God Bless You.

CHAPTER SIX

FAITH IS A CONDITION TO HAVE A RELATIONSHIP WITH GOD

*"Now faith is the substance of things hoped for,
the evidence of things not seen."
Hebrews 11:1*

One of the most precious things before God's eyes in Christianity is Faith. Faith is the dimension in which God can relate to us. He knows that some people only have a little faith, and others may have developed a more mature faith. Faith is written" Pistis," which means belief, the conviction that something is true, belief, fidelity.

Every man on earth is born with a natural faith to believe in something; when something has the correct fountain, faith will produce good results. For example, you may think that a monkey is a God, a cat is a God, but that does not guaranty that if you die, you will go to heaven; It does not provide any instruction on how to have a better life. So, faith must be worked together with instruction. Those instructions are also "conditions."

When those instructions are written, they are called "logos." When the teaching is the voice of God, it is called "Rhema." Rhema words are words that have come by the Spirit of God to your Spirit. It allows us to understand what we see and what we hear. Faith operates like a muscle that stretches out and then relaxes and comes down to normality, which means faith is affected by the outside environment. Your faith will be affected if you do not know how to put the filter of the Spirit on what you see and hear, and the only thing that will make your faith grow more substantial; is to exercise it like a normal muscle.

Often, people have difficulty understanding the concept of faith. This chapter will share ideas and examples that I believe will affirm your knowledge about how faith works.

Faith is like a living, independent organ of the body as a kidney, eyes, and heart. If someone dies, those parts of his body still hold life for a certain period, but if they are transplanted into another person's body, those organs will keep doing the same function for which God created them regardless of the host they are.

So, faith is a seed that grows up like a plant and has its own life. You can be dead spiritually because of difficult circumstances. However, faith is still alive within your Spirit, waiting to spark up by the Spirit of God and be transplanted from the negative body to a positive host, which is you.

That seed needs water to grow and be strong, and the water that feeds your faith is the Word of God. There are other kinds of sources, which means that people who do not know Christ still have faith, genuine faith that has received nutrition to grow even if the waters were not perfectly clean. Those waters can be any spiritual doctrine that sounds good, which builds up discipline, self-control, perseverance, and many other things but will never offer eternal life as the clean water of the Word of God does.

We can say that every human being born is born with a natural faith. When that person knows Jesus, the Holy Spirit gives that person better confidence that is not based on knowledge or experience but in a relationship with God. Also, there are specific individuals that the Holy Spirit gives the gift of faith. *1 Cor. 12:7-9 "Now to each one the manifestation of the Spirit is given for the common good." to another faith by the same Spirit, to another gift of healing by that one Spirit."* Believe it or not, the trials, difficulties, and transitions are the things that sharpen our faith in our mentality but, at the end of the story, when God finishes his process within us, we will be moving into another spiritual dimension.

A real man or woman of God must have that muscle thoroughly trained and exercise; most people exercise every power of the body, but only a few focuses on stretch out the muscle of faith. A good question to ask is, why is my faith not enough to receive what I am asking? Because it is not about how great your faith is, it is about how strong is your relationship with God.

The above verse says that the Spirit gives certain people the gift of faith, which means he will plant a new seed of faith that will grow up more robust than the genuine faith, strong enough to build up the body of Christ and build his kingdom. Do not forget we are new creatures in Christ Jesus.

In the book of *Luke 17:5-6," The apostles said to the Lord, "Increase our faith!" He replied, "If you have faith as small as a mustard seed, you can say to this mulberry tree, 'Be uprooted and planted in the sea,' and it will obey you.*

They thought now that Jesus was going to lay hands on them and release a portion of faith upon their lives, but it was just the opposite. Jesus himself expressed that faith begins in the Spirit of man as a seed the size of the smallest seed of any legume, vegetable, or even fruit; And it can only grow by the opposition. So, faith may change from one season to another like a harvest because faith will always be affected by the outside environment; that is why I often said be careful when listening to negative words. Because words have power, and your faith can be contaminated and will change in a negative direction.

Every tree goes through seasons, and I am sure that our faith should be more vigorous in winter; even if the trees look dead on the outside, they retain so much life on the inside to make it to the next season. So, the one thing that made the tree's roots strong is the challenges of the seasons they went through. So, from today on, please, open your understanding, close your mouth, and stop complaining. Let God finish His word within you.

If you can see your difficulties from a heavenly perspective, you will make your life a lot easier, and you can serve in the Ministry with more joy. Faith is not a condition for God to bless you. Faith is a condition to have a relationship with the Mighty God.

Our trials bring us closer to God only if we love Him with transparency. Opposition is a simple tune-up that sharpens our faith so, the next time we droop about God, our faith would be at the mature level He is expecting to be so we would be able to understand the next step within His divine purpose with our lives.

Let me give you an example. Our kids often want to spend time with us, and often we play, and they feel loved, but when they begin to grow more, they want to play less, ask more questions, and understand things better. That is maturity. What happened with the little kid? His faith just went to another level of maturity naturally. So, he grew in his perspective about the world around him. In other words, God created us to grow, and be mature, so he would be able to release bigger things within our hands. Now, you understand why you have not received what you asked for in your Ministry; everything is about your faith level.

How many times have you asked God to increase your faith? Exactly what He did with his disciples, He will do with you. He will put you through difficulties, but He will never leave you alone because that is how the seed of faith grows. The incredible thing is that the power of that relationship makes our children believe everything we say. They grow up remembering things like "my father told me, I learned from my father such and such." The question is, what makes them believe so strongly the words of instructions we gave them?

The answer is "relationship."

Faith is given when a person is born, and at some point, in life, he must find the fountain of life which gave humankind the seed, which is "Jesus." That is how faith works, like a mustard seed. It is planted within the heart of a man and will reach its full potential by an encounter with God. Hallelujah!

Let me give you some examples of how this works: A famous preacher that God spoke to about receiving a big blessing. God said to him that He would give him an airplane to travel farther and easier to more places worldwide. He took that word and waited. The first thing that he said in his thoughts, "This can't happen right away; by the time that I have everything that is involved, including the landing of the airplane, it will be many years." The main thing is that he was a man that pleased God. He was a man that had a strong relationship with the Holy Spirit; the anointing of God moved with him everywhere he went. Suddenly, he received a phone call. A businessperson offered to give him an airplane; he said he would pay for the insurance, the maintenance, and the pilot every time he needed one. The preacher was without words! He said I guess I need to wait in God to finish the rest. After a week had passed, he received another phone call. An older woman that heard the message was touched by God, and desired to give him a house. He thought he could use that house to buy the land he needed to build the runway. He went to see the home and the location, and it happened that the property that was going to donate the women had enough land for him to build the landing track runway. That was amazing! God is a perfect God. He will always take care of the blessing, details, and things you need so that the blessing does not burden you.

The last thing that God said after He blessed him was, "Son, it was not a problem for me to give you financial blessings, I am The God that owns the gold and silver; the problem was your faith to believe it and to believe that you deserved. God also said, you have set the scale of our relationship too high, that I am pleased to know how thirsty you are after me. I have given you the favor to expand your Ministry to the nations of the world because you have touched my heart. Why did you wait too long to believe that I can give you above and beyond on things you have not even though or ask me for!

It is not only about faith; it is about a relationship. You can work and work as much as you want and never get an increase but, when He desires to bless you based on your relationship, He will open doors that nobody can close. He will give you connections that will change your destiny for good and set you up at the right location, with the right employees, the right people, and even the right spouse to fulfill your destiny. Glory to God!

Your genuine faith will do mighty things when the seed has an encounter with the author. Are you listening to what I am saying! In Matt 8: 6-13, *"Lord," he said, "my servant lies at home paralyzed, suffering terribly." Jesus said to him, "Shall I come and heal him?" The centurion replied, "Lord, I do not deserve to have you come under my roof. But say the word, and my servant will be healed, for I am a man under authority, with soldiers under me. I tell this one, 'Go,' and he goes; and that one, comes and he comes. I say to my servant, 'Do this,' and he does it." When Jesus heard this, he was amazed and said to those following him, "Truly I tell you, I have not found anyone in Israel with such great faith. But the subjects of the kingdom will be thrown outside, into the darkness, where there will be weeping and gnashing of teeth." Then Jesus said to the centurion,*

"*Go! Let it be done just as you believed it would."*

And his servant was healed at that moment." The above verse is a perfect example of how the centurion had great faith, also a good understanding of authority. But only when the faith of that man had a connection with Jesus did his faith produce a miracle. The scripture says that Jesus told him, "Go, let it be done as you believed it would," and his servant was healed, and the miracle happened not by Jesus' Faith but by the centurion's faith.

One of the reasons why the Holy Spirit does not give us all those big blessings that we are still asking God for is because we are more focused on the gifts than the giver of the gifts. We are more focused on the blessing than the blesser, and if we keep in that mentality, our lives are not ready for more. The prodigal son received his blessing when his faith was not ready to receive it, and he ended up losing everything. God is a God of wisdom, and He does not want you to be foolish. He wants to build you up in your faith so you can be ready to qualify for more.

Hallelujah!

Daniel had to have strong faith to understand the mind of God that He should have a better plan for his life when a decree was made that all the people of Israel must be freed out of Babylon and return to rebuild the walls of Jerusalem. That is another perfect example of how important it is to allow our faith to see through God's dimension. Otherwise, we will be arguing with God all the time.

I can tell you through this book that you are in the job where you are for a reason; stop arguing with God. I am sure Daniel did not want to stay with people that worshiped other gods, but he saw through the eyes of the Spirit that it was God's purpose, and he obeyed because obedience counts more than sacrifices.

The bible says in the book of *Hebrews 11:1-3*," *Now faith is confidence in what we hope for and assurance about what we do not see. "This is what the ancients were commended for." "By faith, we understand that the universe was formed at God's command so that what is seen was not made out of what was visible."*

I want to finish this chapter by sharing the above verse. I was taught in faith class that we may not see anything, but we hope that even if we did not see it, it would happen. We do not see in the natural, but we see in the Spirit because faith always sees, but in another sphere, God's dimension is. You know verse three that says," *By faith, we understand that the universe was formed at God's command, so that what is seen was not made out of what was visible"* In the natural eyes, God did not see anything. In God's spiritual dimension, He saw the universe's design and put thought into everything needed. He Calculated the physics, the astronomy involved, and the list will go on, but when He finished, He named his creation and called by its name to be manifested into the earthly atmosphere.

So, faith sees things, but in another dimension, another atmosphere, and based on our more profound relationship with God, we would be able to pull it down from spheres to our natural world. In other words, the mature faith will only see to the glass of the heavenly atmosphere; and if you see it, then you can decree to be manifested in the earth. Remember that Jesus is at the right hand of the Father, interceding for all our needs, everything that we ask the Father in the name of Jesus the Father will give us.

It is time to exercise the muscle of the faith by seeing difficulties with the proper perspective. The first thing that the enemy will always try to block is our faith because if the devil blocks your faith, then he can block your blessings by blocking your relationship with God.

Every time you cannot see in the dimension of God, that means your faith needs to be shaken off. It means the devil who is a liar is bringing schemes to your thoughts to create certain unbelief, and you need to cast down every opposition that is holding your blessings and blinding your spiritual eyes in the name of Jesus. It's written in the word of God *Hebrews 11:6," And without faith, it is impossible to please God, because anyone who comes to him must believe that he exists and that he rewards those who earnestly seek him.* Keep persevering and never give up on your relationship with the Lord. He loves us and wants to release at your feet the things you are asking for with such favor, especially those who understand the power of relationship. Amen

The Author.

CHAPTER SEVEN

THE MENTALITY OF DETERMINATION

"If any of you lacks wisdom, let him ask of God,
who gives to all liberally and without reproach,
and it will be given to him. But let him ask in faith, with no doubting,
for he who doubts is like a wave of the sea driven and tossed by the wind.
For let not that man supposes that he will receive anything from the Lord.
James 1:5-7

One of the most important things after developed faith in God is to recover the King's mind. As I explained in previous chapters, it begins when we exercise determination.

Many believers have gone through difficulties and discouragements and many other negative things in their lives. Still, when they begin to exercise determination, it will bring them to a total change, including their present location, because people who have determination will conquer what they want most of the time.

Statistics show that many people that become wealthy never began with money. They started with one divine idea that came out of nowhere, from God, that gave them the inner assurance that it was a key for their success! Money is not our problem; the lack of determination is our problem, the lack of order, the lack of focus. If this is your case, it is time to stop that disorder and ask God for wisdom; as the apostle, James says, "if anyone has a lock of wisdom, ask God that He will give it to you. "Most billionaires around the world have been in bankruptcy.

A few of them have closed their business because of the lack of revenue. Others lost their wives because of the lack of income. Still, there is one characteristic that all of them have in common. They *never changed the mentality of determination because they knew how to learn from their mistakes and failures; they knew that only good photos came out of the negatives. Are you listening to what I am saying? That is the mentality of determination that makes them stronger every time things did not come the way they planned. It looks like they applied the word of God that says in the book of Proverbs 24:16, "for though the righteous fall seven times, they rise again, but the wicked stumble when calamity strikes."*

If this is your case, consider that God is telling you to be prepared to dream again, to have a new vision about your destiny. Forget the past once forever and reach out by faith to your future as these billionaires did one day in their lives.

One key to obtaining success is to maintain focus until you see results. The other thing is to learn how to wait in God's voice before moving forward. I applied it in my life, and I know it works; **in anything you plan to do in your life,** *always wait for God's approval.* The Bible says in the book of ***Proverbs 16:3, "Commit to the LORD whatever you do, and he will establish your plans."*** God speaks through the Bible directly to your spirit through his prophets, and God speaks through circumstances. He will create a way to be sure you understand His message. For example, when you get many ideas about investing or anything else, always ask yourself, did God approve it?

Let us go deeper. The Bible says in the book of ***Proverbs 19:21," Many are the plans in a person's heart, but it is the LORD's purpose that prevails."*** It is like God is fighting your emotions, thoughts, your feelings to win *His will within you according to His purpose with your life. It is nothin*g on the outside. It is every battle on the inside that God must win to protect you from another failure. No, you are not listening to what the spirit of God is sayi*ng!* God will often say no, or God will say nothing, and the silence of God means a lot, the silence of God is an answer for those that love the Lord.

In the journey of my Christian life, I have learned that God's silence means it is not the right time to do whatever you are planning to do, and sometimes God uses His silence to wake up within us the mind of determination. Why? Because God knows that until the man's mind gets affirmed with character, personality, and judgment about what he wants to do from the beginning to the end, no matter what door God opens, it will be a waste of time.

The Bible says in the book of *James 1:6, 'But when you ask, you must believe and not doubt, because the one who doubts is like a wave of the sea, blown and tossed by the wind".* That is the same when we determine something, believe it, and no doubt it but believe it, feel it, and it will come to pass. Amen! The word determination is written in the Hebrew Aramaic dictionary "Mishpat," which means: a case of decision, judgment, fitness, manner, and plan. If we interpreted the meaning would be paraphrased that determination has to be with a judgment of results in the actions of an individual. Also, it means setting up a plan to be exercised to be put into action; in other words, wisdom to determine decisions.

You can dress up as a king and never act like it. Determination affects our spirit, soul, and body, which means that it affects how we think, feel, and see ourselves. Resolutions can be made for good or bad but, one thing we know for sure is that whatever we determine, it is going to happen. Many times, we choose things too fast, and our destiny becomes affected. Just wait on God, let Him confirm what you already saw in the spirit by the word of God or by a prophet that does not even know you. Still, the main thing is to purpose in your heart, not to make more mistakes that will jeopardize your family. Before closing this precious chapter, let me give you a Biblical example about how important it is to determine things only when God has approved. The book of *2 King 2: 9-14 says: "When they had crossed, Elijah said to Elisha, tell me, what I can do for you before I am taken from you?" "Let me inherit a double portion of your spirit," Elisha replied. "You have asked a difficult thing," Elijah said, "yet if you see me when I am taken from you, it will be yours— otherwise, it will not." As they were walking along and talking together, suddenly a chariot of fire and horses of fire appeared and separated the two of them, and Elijah went up to heaven in a whirlwind.*

Elisha saw this and cried out, **"My father! My father! The chariots and riders of Israel! And Elisha saw him no more. Then he took hold of his garment and tore it in two**. *Elisha then picked up Elijah's cloak that had fallen from him and went back and stood on the bank of the Jordan.* He took the cloak that had fallen from Elijah and struck the water with it. "Where now is the LORD, the God of Elijah?" he asked. When he hit the water, it divided to the right and the left, and he crossed over.

The Bible says that God called Elisha to do more extraordinary things than Elijah. That is what happens today; much authority has been reduced from God's people that have made wrong decisions. It is written in the Hebrew dictionary "Addereth," which means: Glory of God, mantle, cloak, and splendor. The Bible says: in the book of *Hosea 4:6, my people are destroyed from lack of knowledge.*

"Because you have rejected knowledge, I also reject you as my priests; because you have ignored the law of your God, I also will forget your children. Everybody mentions these prophets but never realizes that it never happens in Elisha's ministry to the level of doing the most extraordinary things than Elijah. Why? Because Elisha made a wrong determination now that he received the cloak. Verse 12 says that he tore it in two. *The moment Elisha tore the mantle in two pieces, the power that was through the garment was cut off in half. Elisha develops his ministry only using half of the authority that was delegated through Elijah's garment.* I said it before, our decisions affect our destiny, and God never told Elisha to tear

the garment into two pieces. Elisha was never able to have his disciple that when he finished duties on earth, someone continued with the mantle. He cursed his servant because he lied, condemn a company of forty-two youth because they laugh at him. All of those were wrong decisions. It is time to stop making decisions by emotions when the kingdom of God moves at the level of the Spirit. If we want our lives to change, the first change begins with determining who we are; Also, learning from our past mistakes and use that experience for good in the present. The devil is a liar, and I declare that you will be a solid and mature person by making decisions that will determine to be in the purpose of God.

Overall, people have suffered because they had have determined wrong. Wrong decisions will place you in the wrong location. Remember, money is not your problem. The love for money is the root of every evil thing. God wants you to have money but never love the money more than Him. God wants you to have power but not to kill his people as Elisha did. God wants you to ask for wisdom to make the right decisions if you feel you do not have it. I often told my wife that when I was younger and I made mistakes, it was not a problem because I had plenty of time to make it up, but now that I am older, I have no time to experiment again. It is time to make the right decisions according to God's purpose in our lives. Amen!

God Bless You.

CHAPTER EIGHT

THE BREAKTHROUGH OF THE KINGDOMS

"But, if anyone does not provide for his own, and especially for those of his household, he has denied the faith and is worse than an unbeliever."
1 Tim. 5:8 (RVR60)

ONE OF THE MOST DECEITFUL things that have happened to most Christian leaders worldwide is fighting the battle by themselves. There are no heroes in the heavens, not even Jesus because He never pretended to be one of them; He is the king of kings because the father gave Him that privilege. The Bible says, *"In order that Satan might not outwit us. For we are aware of his schemes." 2 Cor. 6:11 (RVR60)* The enemy is an adversary that constantly is sending arrows against your family to finish you by discouragement, anxiety, or fear. Satan has experience of knowing how to take people out of the front line of their ministries; that is why many servers of the Lord have returned their credentials and go back to regular life because they never ask for help. Remember, there are no heroes in the heavens!

Dear brother and sister, the Ministry's foundation is neither the anointing nor the knowledge of the word of God; it is how strong is the relationship with God and between the family. Multitudes have lost the battle in that area, like king David; He was famous for people's opinions, but inside of the palace not even his wife Michal recognized him as a king; because he did focus on making people happy but no his own family, and today, there are many doing the same thing, especially in the body of Christ. I do not know your present situation, but if you are one of them, consider this chapter as a prophetic voice of God to restore your life!

Many people will not go any farther in the Divine purpose of God just because they missed understanding this principle.

Throughout twenty-eight years of being a Christian, I have seen this deceitful weapon of the enemy be used accurately against God's people, and if this is your case, I declare that it is about to end forever. God does no gives Breakthrough unless there is order in the house. We can fool the congregation, but we cannot fool God; and the reason this book is in your hands; is because God wanted to bless you abundantly above and beyond of what you cannot even imagine, and the first thing that He is asking you to do, is, to be honest, to be transparent with yourself, once forever.

Stop complaining if your kids are not serving God; they know you more than you may know yourself. They do not say so because they love you, but at some point, you will find out that they knew you missed the divine order. The Bible says in the book of Hosea *4:6*, '*my people are destroyed from lack of knowledge. "Because you have rejected knowledge, I also reject you as my priests; because you have ignored the law of your God, I also will ignore your children."* The statistics show that ninety percent of Christian leaders have been betrayed from their right hands on their ministries; it creates that most ministers do not have friends, and when they have problems, they cannot ask for help from anybody because they are constantly judged; that is one more reason to change the perspective tours your wife. Because six thousand five hundred churches are closing to the public every year, and the only thing that every pastor will have at the end, is his family; and mostly your wife would be there for you when things go wrong.

Let me give you some essential perspectives to pay attention to:

The affirmation of your kingdom-Family begins with your wife and your kids' attention.

What qualifies you to receive more are not the results of the outside Kingdom-Ministry, but the results of the inside one.

God has placed a spiritual stop tours the growth of many Ministries because of this matter. God is a God of order, and He preferred to hold a harvest from many to keep you where you are until you have the eyes to see and the humbleness to recognize the need to have a balance between family and Ministry. Stop playing hero with the crow, but losing your family; remember, your wife is not your enemy, do not let the enemy deceit you. She is an instrument of God to bless you and help you reach out to other levels.

Your kids are not your disgrace because they are not part of the chorus or playing an instrument, weak up! Do not let the enemy deceit you; they are your blessing and happiness that God gave you. The fact that your kids and your wife are not active in the Ministry means that they are not ready, and most probably, they are wounded with something that you have done in the past.

Stop blaming God if He did not bless the Ministry; change the perspective to one hundred-eighty degree and reflect on the selfish past heart's priorities. The Breakthrough comes from the inside-out, not from the outside-in.

When a man of God can set up prayer time with his wife, that battle has been conquered. When a man of God sets up a weekly time with his kids, like teaching a Bible study or going for a walk, other ground is conquered. People like that are ready to win any battle that comes ahead against their Ministry, finances, or anything else. They will qualify to receive more. When a family prays united, there is no devil, no curse, not sicknesses that can resist the power of that prayer. Deut. 32:30 *"How could one man chase a thousand, or two put ten thousand to flight unless their Rock had sold them unless the LORD had given them up"?* Hallelujah! Many Christian leaders have fallen down the row or backslide in continuing into their calling because they have not received enough discipleship and have rush into their Ministry without having a solid marriage. A solid marriage sprang up not by accident; it requires a plan, time investment, and order of priorities to affirm our loved ones. People who have understood how important it is to have a plan involving their families in the Ministry will always see good results along the route.

In the book of *Acts 15:36-38, "Paul said to Barnabas, "Let us go back and visit the believers in all the towns where we preached the word of the Lord and see how they are doing." Barnabas wanted to take John, also called Mark, with them, but Paul did not think it wise to take him because he had deserted them in Pamphylia and had not continued with them in work."*

We see in this passage how Apostle Paul was rejecting the Apostle John to go on one of his missionary trips. The Apostle did not see him ready, but he did nothing to encourage him or finish to disciple him or something else; He just rejected him. Sometimes, as fathers, husbands, and teachers, we focus only on the outside world that we do not see the potential that it is in our kids or our wives.

We keep failing the test over and over. The Bible shows that Barnabas took the time to finish discipleship. He took the time to bring the necessary affirmation to his calling and the necessary healing to his rejection.

Now at today's date, if it were not for Barnabas, the Apostle John would not be able to author the book of Revelations, and the Church of Christ would not know where to stand up on these Apocalyptic times that we are going through. Are you listen to what I just said!

When we enjoy listening to messages of the word of God, but not too many people focus on the other side of the story, the process of formation that it takes to be used by God. One of them is the time that they must pay to serve the Lord behind the scenes, time that belong to their wives and kids; As I always say, the anointing never comes free there is a price to be paid behind the pulpit because as higher the calling it is, as more rigid the formation will be.

The server of the Lord must organize priorities about which kingdom is first in the eyes of God; otherwise, the enemy will continue to deceit his heart and emotions, and the results will be no kingdom, no passion, and no Ministry.

The lock of time is a weapon of the enemy to destroy the Pastor's Ministry. To destroy his passion in continue serving the Lord and drain out his strength. The statistics show that most churches that closed to the public were victims of a subliminal attack, and nobody was there to help them!

Nobody asks for help! Everybody wants to keep covering reputation but that is a foolish decision, we all need help, we all need each other, *Jesus could not make it to Golgotha to be crucified by himself, someone had helped him how to get at there. Luks 23:26"* As the soldiers *led him away, they seized Simon from Cyrene, who was on his way in from the country, and put the cross on him and made him carry it behind Jesus.*

Let us be humbled and ask for help before the battle is over, so we avoid being defeat. In *Exodus 17:1014, "So Joshua did as Moses said to him, and fought with Amalek. And Moses, Aaron, and Hur went up to the top of the hill. And so it was, when Moses held up his hand, that Israel prevailed; and when he let down his hand, Amalek prevailed. But Moses' hands became heavy, so they took a stone and put it under him, and he sat on it. And Aaron and Hur supported his hands, one on one side, and the other on the other side; his hands were steady until the going down of the sun. So, Joshua defeated Amalek and his people with the edge of the sword. Then the LORD said to Moses, "Write this for a memorial in the book and recount it in the hearing of Joshua that I will utterly blot out the remembrance of Amalek from under heaven."*

We need to learn how to work as a team, delegate to others, and split responsibilities because we all win at the end of the story.

In the above passage, Mosses did his part, Aaron did his, and Joshua also. The name of God was exalted, and the enemy was defeated; that is how the Lord wants our Ministry and our house to move forward, working as a team.

God did not give you the Ministry to destroy you or your relationship with your family; He gave you the Ministry to rejoiced in it. The wrong decisions that you have made lead you on the wrong path. I have come to tell you by this book that it is time to ask for forgiveness and time to forget about the past. You cannot bring the anointing that was in the past into the present; you cannot continue talking to people about how God used you yesterday; stop living from the visions of yesterday; today is a new day. The Bible says in *Mathew 9:17," Neither do people pour new wine into old wineskins. If they do, the skins will burst; the wine will run out, and the wineskins will be ruined. No, they pour new wine into new wineskins, and both are preserved"* If we want that something good begins to happen in our Ministry, then let us be honest and walk with transparency, so you would be able to see God's Glory within your family, that is changing visitation for habitation! Your kids will speak again with visions and prophecies as before; you will see your wife begin to support you without manipulation, and most important is that people will notice that He oversees the Ministry because it is not about men, but God's agenda. If you have put close attention to the words of this chapter, at this moment tears are pouring from the bottom of your heart, asking God for one more chance, asking the Holy Spirit to be In-Charge, and take control of your life to begin again. I am sure; He will do it because He loves you and is "The God of The Second Chance!"

If you repented from the bottom of your heart, then you will see that the joy will come back home, and the fig tree will bear its fruits like the tree planted next to streams of waters. The Bible says Psalm 1:13 *"Blessed is the man that walked not in the counsel of the ungodly, nor stranded in the way of sinners, nor sited in the seat of the scornful. But his delight is in the law of the LORD; and in his law doth he meditates day and night. And he shall be like a tree planted by the rivers of water, that bringeth forth his fruit in his season; his leaf also shall not wither; and whatsoever he doeth shall prosper".* Glory to God! It is time to turn around your mentality selecting the priorities to work in the correct kingdom. It is time to determine correctly, not more by emotions, but God's voice and I will guarantee you that good changes will begin to happen because when the head is healed, the body is also. The Bible says in *Jer 29:11," For I know the plans I have for you," declares the LORD, "plans to prosper you and not to harm you, plans to give you hope and a future."* What is the next thing that you need to do once you have organized priorities? Spark the passion. In other words, when the family is in order, the next thing is to conquer the land and take back what the enemy has stolen from you, now is your turn, and you need to be passionate about what you are going to do next.

If your family or your congregation does not see your passion, you will not move forward. The Bible says *Exodus 25:2 "Tell the Israelites to bring me an offering. You are to receive the offering for me from everyone whose heart prompts them to give".* Mosses explain the vision that God gave him to build up a tabernacle where His presence will dwell in the ark of the covenant, the scriptures teach us that went the man of God transmit clear the divine plan for his people with the passion for coming and working in the house of the Lord people will give generously because the passion will light them up like a flame of fire. Glory to God!

One of the characteristics of Jesus' Ministry in his three and a half years on earth was that no matter what people told Him, He never lost the passion for continuing walking in obedience to serving the kingdom of God.

The question is why He did never surrender? Because He moved by God's agenda, and that is the agenda that matters. Jesus did not allow anybody to get him out of focus to fulfill his commission. *John 6:39 "And this is the will of him who sent me, that I shall lose none of all those he has given me but raise them up at the last day."*

As a Christian Psychologist, I recommend you focus on working with passion and do not let men's opinion get you out of track because the only thing in heaven that you and I will have to surround accounts with is our family and our Ministry; the rest is a plus.

Maintain focus and do not allow any ungodly influence to distract you from God's agenda. Billy Graham, one of the most famous evangelists in the world, was offered to be a candidate to the presidential campaign with everything paid he answers, "I will never underestimate the calling and the commission that God gave me to fulfill, I have a higher calling the one to be a preacher of the gospel of Jesus Christ." Hallelujah!

Have you ever realized that people criticize you if you have a good car, but they will do the same thing if you have a Junk car? It is time to stop moving your life or your ministry base on people's opinions; the only opinion that should matter for you is the opinion of God. He loves you and wants you to put your heart in the proper order of priorities. It is time to walk in unity with your God and your family and make the proper determinations for your future location.

Let those that live in appearance be full of their financial deaths; that does not please God. He only looks at the heart of the men. The Bible mention in the book of 1 Sam. 16 that God send the prophet Samuel to be anointing one of the sons of Jesse to be a king *16: 6-7: "When they arrived, Samuel saw Eliab and thought, "Surely the LORD's anointed stands here before the LORD." But the LORD said to Samuel, "Do not consider his appearance or his height, for I have rejected him. The LORD does not look at the things people look at. People look at the outward appearance, but the LORD looks at the heart."*

When you read the gospels of Jesus, He was always working in the things of the kingdom. He was healing someone, he was walking to deliver another person, and He was in the boat through the night trying to go somewhere. What happens when someone is putting his faith into actions? The answer is straightforward, **the kingdom of God will be manifested with favor.** What happens when someone brings the necessary healing to his wife and kids for things that he should not say and time that belongs to them? *The anointing will double when the man of God is behind the pulpit. Remember, the message does not begin when you step up to preach. In the pulpit, your message finished because your message did already start when you prioritize your family.*

You may say to me, but I have done that, and nothing has happened! Well, dear brother, this is something that you need to know *nothing of the promises of the word of God will be fulfilled on earth unless we pray and do warfare. Jesus said, my house will be call house of pray. Why?*

Because prayer is the electricity of the Spirit of God, it is the power of love that gives your spirit the fresh passion within your heart to continue to move forward. Without passion, there is not marriage that lasts. Promotion does not come because of the level of your anointing; it comes because you are passionate for God and have a balance between your family and your Ministry. The level of passion that Jesus put into his Ministry provoked that He only needed three and half years to do his commission on earth. Are you listening!

The kingdom mentality should be reinforced with passion because people who have passion will encourage others positively to do the same. I meet a pastor that came from Great Britain, and he has one of the biggest congregations in his country. Every pastor asks him, what did he do? He humbly answers, I only focus on disciple and put on those disciples the passion in my teachings to create the need for them to disciple others, and the passion was placed so strong by the Spirit of God that they went out to find the souls!

The devil has played a game of discouragement with many Pastor, Ministers, and leaders worldwide; he knows that the Ministers who have lost their passion for what they do will be the next church or the next evangelistic center in line closing the doors. I cancel every sublime message in your life that is locking the passion of the new beginning in the name of Jesus!

I was doing tremendous warfare the other day, and the Holy Spirit spoke to me and said, son, I want you to know that there are hundreds and hundreds of blessings that have been retained on heavens that belong to you and are about to be released onto your feet.

Surprisingly, I told the Lord, why hundreds? I cannot believe that devil has stolen so much. He said a few belong to you, many from your father, and a lot from your Grandfather, but now, they belong to you!

Psalm. 79:12 (NIV). And return to our neighbors sevenfold into their bosom their reproach with which they have reproached You, O Lord" I declare that the enemy has to return everything that belongs to your generation.

God is a God that sees hundreds of years in only one divine plan with one generation. The plan that He started with Abraham He continued with Isaac and finished with Jacob. He says: I am the God of Abraham, Isaac, and Jacob, the God of the covenant. *Psalm 105:8-10 "He remembers his covenant forever, the promise he made, for a thousand generations. The covenant he made with Abraham, the oath he swore to Isaac. He confirmed it to Jacob as a decree, to Israel as an everlasting covenant"* **To you, I will give the land of Canaan as the portion you will inherit** There is an inheritance for you in your children and the moment that you get on the front raw his covenant with you will shine again, the covenant to bless you extravagantly that you will be astonished.

Hallelujah!

I also want you to remember that the blessings come to your feet, which means that your present location must walk according to God's agenda. Elisha received the double portion of the spirit of Elijah because he was in the correct city at the right location. *Are you listening!* From today on, let the Holy Spirit guide your steps, let him speak to you but also in the hearts of your wife and kids before to do changes that made involved God's purpose, especially with your family. Let us determine right!

God Bless!

CHAPTER NINE

DESTROY DECEITFULNESS BY OBEDIENCE

"And I saw three unclean spirits like frogs come out of the mouth of the dragon and out of the mouth of the beast, and out of the mouth of the false prophet. For they are the spirits of devils, working miracles, which go forth unto the kings of the earth and the whole world, to gather them to the battle of that great day of God Almighty."
Rev 16:13-14

THERE IS A DAILY BATTLE in every man and woman of God. Some of you deal with depression, others with anxiety, fear, and insecurity, and other spiritual leaders are attacked with deceitful thoughts and prophetic words that never came from God. Whatever direction you struggle with, there are two realities that I am about to tell you in this small chapter.

First, everything begins in your mind; the way you think determines the way you are and the direction you are going to take; your decisions will create your destiny. The first enemy it is in your mind. Today, the first thing every spiritual leader should watch is within themselves. You can lose a battle in the outside world but still being challenged for tomorrow's match. Because if your mind still focuses, one day you will win again! The worse battle that any person of God can lose is the battle of their mind.

The second reality we should concern about is finding how things happened or when the enemy attacked and made us lose the battle? As you see in the above verse, each of them, the dragon, the beast, and the false prophet, bursts out frogs from their mouths, spirits of false miracles and false prophecy. Still, the characteristic is that they are unclean spirits; I always say that a pitch of clean water only needs one drop of dirty water to be contaminated. Are you listen to what I am saying? You did not remember who lay hands on you that you did not know the fountain and all the sudden your life took another direction.

Dear brother, this is a severe issue. The verse above says the first attack will come against the kings of the earth. Which are you and I; we are the first target then the whole world! The devil is recruiting an army of deceitful people, and we need to act now and watch upon ourselves on every prophetic word and every vision that we see. Otherwise, as the Bible says, my people are destroyed for the lack of knowledge.

We often wonder to find the root of a problem in our business or our ministries; I have come to tell you by this chapter that I have seen many brothers finding their answers throughout this book. Here is the root of many problems, "frog devils giving unclean visions by deceitfulness."

The enemy will take advantage and bit us down the road many times, especially when we are more sensitive and tired. I am utterly sure that the enemy has stolen so much from your life that sometimes we desired to forget about it and let the thoughts of the enemy keep moving forward into our minds. Still, as much as we tried to fight the battle, we lost it for the lack of knowledge. People do not realize how important it is to renew our thoughts. I called spiritual cleansing to make the decisions at the right time for the right reason.

In the same way, our body needs to be purged to maintain good digestion, so our mentality! A time for fasting should be something for you to consider while approaching God; that is spiritual cleansing. Unclean people love company in the same way as misery and poverty do not like to be alone. The most unclean people that I know are the ones that keep jumping from church to church; they are unfaithful with their spiritual fathers; those people are jars that carry on fealty water. They lived from prophetic meetings to prophetic warfare and finished in cosmetic appearance; they live in poverty because

God will provide, they never find a job because the Lord has not told them to do so, and the list will go on. Dear pastor, be careful with this kind of influence in your Ministry; it is time to put the house in order and reach our breakthrough!

It is not God's will that someone serves the Lord in the Ministry and does not provide for his own family with responsibility (1Tim. 5:8).

You only need one word from God to be touch in the way you think to transform your destiny. Are you listening to what I am saying!

The enemy sends his arrows when we are exhausted. That is the only way that everything goes directly to our minds; when fear and depression overtake you, as a Christian Psychologist, I can say that those are vulnerable moments in which deceitful thoughts overtake your mind.

Whoever, if the enemy can have your ideas, then, easily may have the keys of the Kingdom Mentality that remains within you!

The third reality is that God is still in control of your destiny regardless of your present situation. Remember, the enemy is under your feet by the power of the resurrection of our Lord Jesus Christ, so never forget the authority of Jesus that there is within you (Eph. 1:17-24).

People do not walk in obedience because deceitfulness is blocking their minds. How to overcome deceitful thoughts? The Bible says, *"And they overcame him by the blood of the Lamb, and by the word of their testimony, and they loved not their lives unto the death."* Rev. 12:11 (NIV)

Persuade to be fed with a fresh word of God and assemble in the church as the Bibles command us to do. People who assemble daily are cover under the blood of Jesus, so everything is protected. Still, the anointing of God will spark the fire of the Spirit to keep you testifying about the Lord. Remember, false prophets never submit under any spiritual authority; they said that God reveals to them everything, and that is wrong! We need to *watch upon our thoughts and visions because we still humans; as the above verse says, we overcome the enemy by the lamb's blood and by our testimony. It is time to present ourselves before God, accountable!*

I have seen churches and ministers getting out of track walking and circles and getting nowhere because of a wrong mentality. You cannot eat every spiritual thing given to you if you do not know the fountain. People who assemble understand communion's power; that is the first thing to do to overcome false visions or prophetic words that God never spoke. In the Book of Mic. 3: 5-7, it says, *"This is what the LORD says: "As for the prophets who lead my people astray, they proclaim 'peace' if they have something to eat but prepare to wage war against anyone who refuses to feed them." The seers will be ashamed, and the diviners disgraced. They will all cover their faces because there is no answer from God."*

As I said in this chapter, every new level is a new devil. Deceitful is the stronghold that Satan is and will use to take back many chosen people of God. Deceitfulness is something that not too many spiritual leaders talk about, but this is a dangerous weapon of the enemy for the end times. Why?

Because deceitfulness begins by affecting our minds, it also affects how we see things and how we understand them; there is a need today in all Christianity to have a new mentality to deal with this new world order.

Nothing happens by accident; every problem in the present began with something in the past, and the only thing that produces change it is doing something directly to cut it off from the root. The gap time of uncertainty is the space where the enemy works hard in our minds, and if we keep our minds focused regardless of our present situation, we still winning the battle and be more than conquers in

Jesus Christ. Amen

In the book of Genesis, because of disobedience, Adam and Eve lose the natural privilege to hear God's voice; the second thing they lose was their territory. It seems like every spiritual mistake we make is used by the enemy to steal our position of authority and steal our finances. Adam and Eva had pay with the most value and beautiful place on earth," the garden. All of that happened because of the enemy's deceitful weapon, a sweet voice to your ears that make sense to your understanding but came from an unclean fountain; frogs that came out of the serpent's mouth.

The book of *Judges 6:1; 5 says, "The Israelites did evil in the eyes of the LORD, and for seven years he gave them into the hands of the Midianites. They produced their livestock and their tents like swarms of locusts. It was impossible to count them or their camels; they invaded the land to ravage it."* The whole nation of Israel was deceitful by the enemy; I wonder how nobody the eyes must see that the land that God gave them was taken from their hands; it took decades to get to the promised land. Because when a leader is infected, then easily hundreds, thousands, and ten-thousands would also be.

When the head of the house is healed, the family is also, but if the head of the house is deceitful, it will also be the rest of the family, so when disobedience begins before God, we will see adverse outcomes. If you speed up in your car and violate the traffic rules, you must pay with money; if you are mistaken paying your taxes to the Government, they charge you for the lack of knowledge regardless of your innocence. So, "the golden rule *it's to know the root that has trap the past so that we can unleash the blessings in our present.*

In the above verse, everybody knows the root, but nobody wants to stand up and raise in the name of Jehovah! Why? Because they knew that God determined seven years because of disobedience. In other words, we might cast down the enemy, we may fast and intercede, but when God already decreed seven years of discipline, no matter what we do, nothing is going to change. The important thing we can learn from this is that God moves in seasons. It is so important to know the season of the month on the first day of the calendar. Because the river of His blessings will continue the entire month into the same divine plan, that is why each month has a number, and each number has a meaning. So, you comprehend that God moves and Spheres in the heavens and within Seasons in the earth.

It is time to wake up! And open the eyes of the Spirit, especially if you have a calling from God; people are years and years trying to make something work, locations, but the time passes by, and there is no fruit, no harvest. Why? Because we need to discover what God has done in specific cities and certain nations. For example, the Haiti earthquake was not by accident. What happened in Japan with the tsunami was not by accident, and what it is about to occur in the United States will not be by accident; God will use judgments on Nations and cities to call people to repent, but they do not listen. Stop wasting time and money upon regions that the only things that will make them change are when the judgments of God pass by. Weak up and be more effective in showing results within your ministry or missionary work.

The Bible never mentions exactly that one leader oversaw the promised land; it seems like everyone was responsible for their own decisions. That means the plan of deceitfulness took its time but ended, affecting them all with frog-devils-of-deceitfulness. Same as Eva use to be a friend-talker with the serpent in the garden until deceitfulness took place. Deceitfulness never happens by accident; you get familiar with that spirit. The fact that you saw dirty water filling up the jar and desired to drink some of it. So, your spiritual eyes got blind, your spiritual ears got plugged, and your disobedience made you lose your territory. That is why our present situations are consequences of the deceitfulness of the past. The land that the Medians took was the promised land of milk and honey that God gave the Israelites since He set them free out of Egypt. I believe that you maintain the authority of your territory by walking in obedience, knowing the roots of your environment, and keep in spiritual warfare. Because nothing happens until pray it is involved.

Dear brother and sister, the reason that this book it is in your hands means God wants to give you one more chance! He wants to give you back all the territory that the devil has stolen from you. I have come to tell you that the time of your seven years of discipline; is over!

I have come to tell you *that the worse it is over in the best is yet to come, is time to shake off the dust out of your eyes and look again, because everything that devil has stolen from you, he will have to return it seven times seven in the name of Jesus. Hallelujah! I declare new beginnings in your life. I decreed you are the head and not the tail. I declare favor in every new thing that God will give you from today further. I declare that every door that was close by satanic forces is open in the name of Jesus. I declare that every Spirit of deceitfulness and confusion is casting down in the name of Jesus. Amen and amen!*

God Bless you!

CHAPTER TEN

"RECOVER YOUR TERRITORY."

"I am the God of Bethel, where you anointed a pillar and where you made a vow to me. Now leave this land at once and go back to your native land."
Gen 31:13

THEN LABAN SAID TO JACOB, "Because you *are* my relative, should you, therefore, serve me for nothing? Tell me, what *should* your wages *be?*" Now Laban had two daughters: the elder's name *was* Leah, and the name of the younger *was* Rachel. Now Jacob loved Rachel, so he said, "I will serve you seven years for Rachel, your younger daughter." So, it came to pass in the morning that beholds, it *was* Leah. And he said to Laban, "What is this you have done to me? Was it not for Rachel that I served you? Why then have you deceived me?" And Laban said, "It must not be done so in our country to give the younger before the firstborn. "Fulfill her week, and we will give you this one also for the service which you will serve with me still another seven years." Gen 29:15-27

Jacob worked extremely hard for many years for his wives, but he was a victim of abuse by his father-inlaw. His Father –In –Law prospered while Jacob remained poor. Why? Because He was not in the territory that God had set up for him to be blessed but, when God is about to do something in your life, he will give you the right direction where to go. Based on the above verse, that time of prosperity was about to begin for Jacob, and I believe it is about to start for you. Dear reader, this last chapter of this precious book "Kingdom Mentality.' I have come to tell you in this chapter as God said to Jacob, paraphrasing the above verse, "The God of Light (Bethel) where you made a covenant is telling you to leave the place you are, and go back to the place one day you began."

I always ask why? Because every man and woman of God has a territory that God preordained from heaven, and at the appointed time, your feet will touch that ground that was predestined for you to receive your harvest.

I have come to tell you that today, God has remembered you. He has remembered to take you out of the anonymous secret place of processing and put you in places of honor. He is about to open doors that nobody can close and give you the divine connections that you need in the land that He has prepared for you so He can fulfill promises one day made to your parents and Grandparents before you pass away. Glory to God!

Gen 2:10 "A river watering the garden flowed from Eden; it was separated into four headwaters **from there.** God is so powerful to make the land of the garden fruitful with only one river. I have seen many nations be supported by just one river, but the fact that God created four rivers to bless the garden of Adam and Eve means more than a simple river. A river is a stream of water that has life in it. When we see that God desired to multiply the waters of the same river to feed life to all the threes of the garden, it means that such territory was relevant for God.

Four rivers surrounding the garden are more than enough. Because the moment that you desire to come back to the land that God told you to do everything that one day belongs to you, it will come back when you get to the correct location. Israel is a blessing, but Jewish travel to pray from the wall of prayers. Why? Because location means position, and position means authority.

The question is, why four rivers? The answer is that God was assuring that the territory He chose for His creation would never run out of life, would never dry out of waters. When God gave such an environment to Adam, He gave them all the wealth and prosperity that every king deserves. The beauty of the garden, the gold and precious stones underneath the ground, plus the grace to enjoy a relationship with the Almighty God; will make them happy! Four rivers represent four streams of income.

Everything works by conditions. Let me tell you what that is. Conditions are foundational requirements that, according to the Scriptures, must be fulfilled to receive the promises of God. Now, the condition to enjoy what God was about to do was to get to his father's land; prosperity will last longer when we obey His conditions; because behind every promise of God, there is a demand to fulfill.

Glory to God!

The Bible has more than five thousand promises, but there is always a condition before every promise in the entire Bible. Read the Bible carefully, and you will notice that there is a condition somewhere else before He gives you something. Let us see some examples: The requirement to go and receive a promised land, a territory of prosperity for Abraham, was to leave by faith his own land and obey his calling.

The condition to enjoy the garden was not to eat from the tree of Good and Evil.

The condition over the people of Israel to retain authority upon the promised land was neither to worship other gods nor to join with other pagan nations.

The condition of Deuteronomy twenty-eight with all those blessings was to hear and obey the commandments given through the prophets. The condition of the promise of salvation is to recognize the sacrifice of Jesus Christ upon the cross.

The condition to receive a harvest has planted a seed.

The condition to have a real family is to be faithful to your wife and care for the woman He gave you. And I can go on and on, but I believe it is clear. God can activate in your life favor to receive His promises, but He will be watching upon those who are fulfilling his conditions and nothing else. In other words, it is time to talk less and do more by demonstrating better obedience.

The Christian life becomes easier when we understand His conditions. *For example, if you want to be loved, you must love others; if you want people to invite you to place, do the same first. From today on, every time you see that something you asked God has not come to your feet, meditate, and find out what condition you missed to fulfill, then do it. You will see the blessing because His answers are abundantly above and beyond your imagination!* Every time man calls upon God from the right location, God will always respond from the territory that God has given him.

The moment that Adam and Eve failed, the first thing God did was to call him. "Adam, where are you?"

It may sound phony to know that God, who is all knowledgeable, was calling him, but because Adam and Eve were transformed from a Glorious body to a carnal body, God did not recognize them. That appearance of fear by sin and lies in their words and hearts was nothing like He created. In other words, sin has made many people lose their territory. Sin has made many like Jacob flee from the land that belongs to them; those years that Jacob was out of his land, the devil allowed his father-in-love to take advantage of his destiny. Now, it is over! It is time for your turn around, and the enemy must return everything that belongs to you!

Now vines that you did not plant and houses that you never built up to have to be transferred to your name because you are a son that God has remembered to give you the blessings that belong to you, your father, and your Grandfather. Glory to God! Every time we sin, we lose the authority that God gave us in the territory that He placed us. God wants for every prosperous man to have four sources of income and not only one. Living from paycheck to paycheck is not a kingdom mentality. Every river is a stream of income; four rivers will protect you from any financial crisis in this economy.

I declare upon you, dear brother, or sister, that you will buy houses with a little bit of money. I declare that when many people begin to migrate from one state to another looking for a better opportunity, you will rise to repossess what belongs to you.

Hallelujah!

I explained in this book; prosperity begins from the inside-out and not from the outside-in, so you understand that your location is as crucial as the foundation of your faith.

Four rivers surrounded the land was wisdom. When a man fails to God, the ground is cursed, and the rivers and everything in them began to wither and die. Your present situation results from your past mistakes. So, we must watch to walk in obedience.

If God told you to go back to your native land, do it! Why do I say this? Because I know He is getting ready to bless you powerfully with divine ideas to bring extravagant prosperity upon your life, your kids, your family, and your business. It is the last chance to return to your territory, the one that has your name on it. Have you ever wondered, those pastors that open a church in a particular region, and their churches became filled with thousands of members within a few years? The answer is, they came back to the land that belongs to them, as Jacob Did. Please, do not miss His voice this time. Pay attention to these words now so that you will not suffer later!

The word of God says, *"And now, Israel, what does the LORD your God ask of you but to fear the LORD your God, to walk in obedience to him, to love him, to serve the LORD your God with all your heart and with all your soul." Dt. 10:12 (NIV)*

I would be wasting my time authoring this book if I did not include this chapter of faith and obedience because it is God's desire for you to get back on track with the mentality of the king that you deserve. When your heart is ready to obey God's voice, there are not streams of income that will change who you are. The word "obey" means in the Hebrew dictionary" to perceive by hearing, understanding, yielding to obey, and discern.

From today on, be ready to obey only the words of the Lord that will come to your spirit. If He tells you to dream again or expand your dreams, just do it.

For example, someone has a supermarket, that person can easily open a bakery or a restaurant because of all the products that the restaurant needs, the supermarket has them. He can also open a checkcashing store that only needs to have one router connected to the internet and verify that the account is legal and has funds in it. Still, funds can be rotated from the other business's cash flow, if needed, and the money continues to multiply. Remember, the one who had the ten talents was the one who received the one that did nothing with the one talent. Ask God for divine ideas to multiply what you have in your hands. Someone had the crazy idea to fed five thousand people without counting their wives and children, but eventually, the miracle happened because obedience counts more than sacrifices.

Glory to God!

If everything keeps going well, buy gold. If you buy gold now and retain it for at least five years, I can guaranty you that your investment will triple, quadruple, or even more; if one business dries out, the other three remain to produce income. One river might be income for your house and expenses; other for your kids' college; other for a retirement savings plan, and the other for investments. Are you listening to what I am saying?

As I explained in one of the chapters before, restoring the Ministry of Kings and priests. I did explain more about extending your mentality to believe that you qualify for more. Repeat, *I do qualify for more!*

If you were asking God for confirmation to have another river of income, the good news is considered these words a divine God's will for you to dream again. If the income never changes your personality, then four rivers of income will never replace the love of Jesus within your heart!

It is time to make a business plan and move forward in those business' ideas that He gave you. If most of the ministers consider these words, I believe that Holiness will rise like an eagle's wings within your life. I said High level because many spiritual leaders are not telling the truth to people in their congregations because they are afraid that people will leave their churches. God is your provider; if He calls you, He will provide for you. Fear not; He is with you.

Money is a paper that society placed a value on it; that currency will not go to heaven; put your eyes on God first, and favor will come to you in everything you do.

Stop scratching the kitchen cabinets trying to get some coins to put gas in your car. Because only until tomorrow will you get pay. Stop living from the government food stamps when the word of God says, *"But thou shalt remember the LORD thy God: for it is he that giveth thee power to get wealth, that he may establish his covenant which he sworn unto thy fathers, as it is this day." Deut 8:18 (NIV)* Food stamps can be a temporary solution for somebody, but your mind must try to get out of it as soon as possible; that is not how God created you to live. People need to understand that with your job alone, you cannot do much. From today on, ask God to release his power of ideas that produce within you the ability to make your wealth, the ability to generate income. It is time to cray out for your four streams of income. The COVID-19 is not the season to complain to God; instead, it is the opportunity to repossess land and houses that others are selling cheap because of fear. It is time to press on for your blessing and see your four rivers of income! Now, what is the condition that God gives you to prosper the business ideas that are about to come? *Deut 8:19-20 "If you ever forget the LORD your God and follow other gods and worship and bow down to them, I testify against you today that you will surely be destroyed. Like the nations the LORD destroyed before you, so you will be destroyed for not obeying the LORD your God."* I do sound rude, but believe me, I have been in abundance, and I have been in the necessity. I have rushed to make decisions based on my experience, based on what my family or friends said, but I forgot to listen for His voice, presuming that I knew how to handle it myself. I have lost many things, and I do not want the same thing to happen to you. The main thing we need to do is to walk in obedience. Obedience is a secret weapon that the devil cannot resist. If you do not want to hear the truth about things in your life, then let me tell you there is a white elephant in the living room of your life that, at some point, someone will have the courage to tell you the truth about yourself, your marriage, and your broken Ministry. The Bible says, "Then you will know the truth, and the truth will set you free." John. 8:32 (NIV).

God is using this book to tell you things you do not want to hear. For example, in the following passage, you may understand me better about the white elephant. I want to tell you this: Many times, we have family members or friends that we are remarkably close to, but that does not mean that they should be part of your business, your divine ideas, or your new projects. If they do not belong with you in that company, nothing they do will bless the company. In other words, the white elephant that has been affecting you are the people that surround you that do not belong there. And your wife has told you that before, and you did not listen! I heard the voice of the Spirit saying, "Brother, sometimes the love that you have for your brother is not the same that he has for you. What you wish for him to be might not be what he wants for you. He is the white elephant preventing your business from reaching the next level. And until you change the way you think, you will not go any farther.

The Bible says in the book of *John 12:37-41, "Even after Jesus had performed so many signs in their presence, they still would not believe in him." Why?* Because when the wrong people surround you, then you are in the wrong location. For God to bring Jacob to his territory, he processed his faith first. Do not forget, "Location is as important as your faith." For God to bring you to your territory, He must bring your faith to the next level. He may speak to you through this book about many things that have nothing to do with money, investments, or connections but only with your mentality; because the way you think affects the way your faith sees things.

There is something vital that everybody with a dream, a vision, or a goal to accomplish things needs to understand. How does your faith see things? The passage just mentioned explains this topic. The prophet Isaiah saw by faith in the present something that was going to happen in the future. Let me paraphrase using the term network. *"The network of heavens allowed seeing a video to Isaiah about the darkness of unbelief that will affect the world in the end times."* Because of the increased percentage of unbelief in most humankind today, most Christians, ministers, and businesspeople should pay attention to the four rivers of prosperity. Like I said, your present location matters!

Adam was placed on earth at the right time, which means God prepared everything for him, the trees with fruits to eat, the land, the animals, the sun, the ground, and its harvest in the perfect location. In other words, He prepared our territory, *and the only thing that we needed to show Him, it is faith,* because the atmosphere of the garden contained waves of faith like electricity. Are you listening to what I am saying?

Getting back to our verse, even if he was the son of the living God, the one performing miracles in front of them, people still did not believe in Him. The Bible says in the gospels that Jesus could not do many miracles in His city because of unbelief. *Mark 6:4-6 "But Jesus said to them, "A prophet is not without honor except in his own country, among his relatives, and in his own house." Now He could do no mighty work there, except that He laid His hands on a few sick people and healed them. And He marveled because of their unbelief. Then He went about the villages in a circuit, teaching.* What did Jesus do? He recognized the white elephant within his people and saw his reality. What was that? No matter how much love he had for Bethlehem to bring them to the light of salvation, the darkness of unbelief; Made Jesus understand that He was trying to perform miracles in the wrong location. Your location matters! I was doing good business in New Jersey, but all my family was in Florida, so I desired to move from my location, where God had blessed me to be close to my family. I was there for one and a half years, and nothing good financially happened to me. The atmosphere, the beaches, and the parks, everything was beautiful, but from the moment that I got there, I did not have peace about it. I had to use all the savings I made for three years to cover the mortgage of two houses I bought. After eighteen months, I had to return to

New Jersey because I was struggling financially.

When I moved back to my territory, the land that God had set up in heaven for me, many doors began to be opened within the same week. God has a marked region for his people. If they understand this principle and walk in obedience, their lives should be improved spiritually, financially, and their marriages would be more robust from Glory to Glory!

Most of the problems begin when men see things with their natural eyes and human understanding. When I did that and moved to Florida, I was surrounded by business with the wrong people, and no matter how many connections I made, nothing worked out for me; nothing supernatural took place during those months. In the end, I knew that the gates of the heavens were close. I said to you that what protects your rivers of prosperity is your obedience. I am not talking about tithes and offerings only, but I am talking about obedience to His voice.

Obedience to his voice is the level where your supernatural faith acts. It is a level between you and God and has nothing to do with anyone else's opinion.

Let me tell you something, dear brother, or sister, that is reading this book. You have a landmarked as God marked His. *"There, the angel of the LORD appeared to him in flames of fire from within a bush. Moses saw that though the bush was on fire, it did not burn up. So, Moses' thought, I will go over and see this strange sight—why the bush does not burn up. When the LORD saw that he had gone over to look, God called him from within the bush, Moses! Moses! And Moses said, Here I am. Do not come any closer, God said. Take off your sandals, for the place where you are standing is holy ground." Exod. 3:2-5 (NIV).*

It is time for everyone that has a dream to conquer, a vision to develop, a goal to be accomplished, to set up limits to your territory as God did for His! It is time to know your limitations. Remember, not every door that opens for you is coming from God. The devil can open doors to distract you and get you off track. The enemy comes to kill, to steal, and to destroy. Still, Jesus has come to bring you eternal life, to give you houses that you did not build up, opportunities, divine connections, and give you all the desires of your heart when you remain in the territory that He blessed for you from the very beginning.

If God has marked his territory, you need to go and keep the city that you want to conquer in the name of Jesus. When you mark a territory God has given you, you must anoint the streets and go to each corner from north to south and east to west. You must rent any vehicle of transportation and bless the heavens up in the air. That way, you are moving in the strong faith of believing that all the business, souls, and divine connections will come to you. Hallelujah! From this point of view, you must move by faith and see yourself from the perspective that He sees you! It is time to forget about mans' opinions and focus on God's opinion. It is time to believe in yourself and forget yesterday's failures; let the past success be out of your heart and begin to work for your present's new dreams and goals.

The word "sees" translates from the Hebrew dictionary: "To see with the eyes, to see with the mind, to perceive, to contemplate, to discern with understanding, to look and to observe." In other words, you can see problems with your physical eyes, but they are already taken care of by God. He will show it to your spiritual eyes because that is what the word "see" means, and that is how God wants you to see circumstances. See in the spirit what He showed you first, and you will see every detail in that dimension of how He took care of your needs!

You will regain your territory by allowing your faith to see in another dimension. Why do I say this? Because as you know, every time you are going to do something new, a significant opposition will begin, and the only thing that will make you move forward is faith!

When you believe what God has shown you, that vision takes place within your understanding, and your faith doubles because your natural faith joins with your spiritual faith. Your genuine faith moves by understanding, but your spiritual faith moves by what God shows you or speaks to you by the word of God. When you read the word of God, your natural faith feeds your understanding, and your spiritual faith keeps feeding the new creation in Christ until it bears out like a volcano. Are you listening to what I am saying!

When you receive a prophecy, remember, it is a confirmation that affirms understanding. Also, the perspective of the genuine faith. Because most of all time, God used the prophet to confirm something that He already spoke to your spiritual faith before, but you did not understand.

The Bible says in the book of Judges 6:1 that the angel of the Lord visited Gideon in times of difficulty, spiritual and financially, and the Lord says to him, *"mighty warrior,"* but He did not believe it. Remember that in those days when the angel of God visited someone, that was a big deal, that was a privilege, but it did not affect Gideon because so many bad things had happened to him, he had a wrong opinion about God.

There are many people today wounded in their hearts against God, like Gideon. They blame God for bad things that have happened to them. When someone is soul-wounded, the root of bitterness blocks their faith, and even if heaven visited them today, they would not respond with the correct attitude. When we must move forward in life and try to be better financially, no matter what we do, sometimes, it seems like nothing moves forward. For example, no matter if you give your tithes and offerings on the church side, it looks like something is holding your blessings, even many Ministers still in the same boat financially. The reality is that there is a white elephant in the living room of your house that nobody wants to talk about it. Is time to fix up your mess!

Your faith will not work until you confront your works. The Bible says, by your fruits, you will know them. (Mat.7:-17-20). Everything you began to do and never finished means you are no ready to do business with God! Mediocracy is a friend of poverty! Stop asking God to bless you financially while you still struggle with bad habits of procrastination.

Stop complaining to God about things He was supposed to do and did not do for you. If you want God to manifest in your life, let us change the concept about Him. He is love forever! The Bible says that Jesus could not do many miracles in his city because there was no faith. Why? Because they saw the son of the carpenter, the son of Mary, but they did not see the man of God. You must forget about the past and begin to fire up your faith! Jesus was discouraged, but it did not stop Him from doing the work of God. It is time to provoke God by bow down and pray, lifting a Holy atmosphere of worship, regardless of your present situation. The atmosphere of faith is like a cloud that moves up in heaven to whatever place you move here on earth and will give you the peace to make the right decisions.

Faith is something spiritual that bears out of your life, like waves of electricity. Faith takes from your spirit the things you want to happen, puts your present location in the future, and moves on your behalf. One of the things in which God commits to bless his people is when He sees faith. Our God is a God that relates with people that believe in Him. Every promise of the Scriptures is waiting on your confession to give you access by faith from the earthly side to the heavenly side.

A man who has been healed in his faith about yesterday's failures should not be afraid to covenant with God. He should not be scared to ask for more rivers of income or more territory because when it is time to ask God, He will hear your prayers and come down and set you free, just as He did with the people of Israel in Egypt.

"Jabez cried out to the God of Israel, "Oh, that you would bless me and enlarge my territory! Let your hand be with me and keep me from harm so that I will be free from pain." And God granted his request." 1 Cron. 4:10 (NIV)

That is one of the simplest prayers that I have seen in the Bible, but when it mentions the word territory, it puts us back to our topic; Adam had his territory and lost it because of disobedience. The people of Israel had their territory, and they lost it for seven years because they did evil before God. God had his territory when His angel manifested to Moses, and He did protect His territory of Holiness.

It is time for you to appreciate what God has given you and walk in obedience to his voice, move in faith and ask for more. If you notice, Jabez did not lose what God gave him, and because of that, He passed the test to be a good steward, so he qualified for more.

The Bible says whoever is faithful in the little things he will be faithful also in the big stuff, which happened to Jabez. I want you to ask for more, ask for more streams of rivers, ask for more forgiveness about the past things. The Bible says, *"Until now, you have not asked for anything in my name. Ask, and you will receive, and your joy will be complete." John 16:24 (NIV). The father is saying, ask me for anything, and give it to you because there is no difference between you and Jabez. The God of Jabez is the same God of you and me, and He will bless us suddenly!*

God said to Jacob, and He says to you," I am the God of Bethel, where you anointed a pillar and where you made a vow to me. Now leave this land at once and go back to your native land.' Gen 31:13 Move forward to recover your territory and never look back. As Jacob did, He took his wives and moved to the city of his father, and God began to bless him because He is a God of Covenant. He often holds things that will distract you from leaving the land that never blessed you but bringing you back into your entire territory.

Elisha received what he wanted because his faith was ready. Gideon did not understand because his faith was affected by the wrong opinion that he had about God. Jabez did a simple prayer, but it was about extending his territory, and God did it because when He sees faith, he will open the windows of heaven with favor and more favor. Today, most kings in the body of Christ are in need to renew their minds. Be part of the new prophetic generation that the Holy Spirit is forming during this Apocalyptic time. Let us move forward!

God Bless You!

The Kingdom Mentality is a book that God put in my heart a long time ago. I knew it was the perfect will of God for me to author this book, but I was waiting for God's perfect timing so that it could be released in the right season.

Many people are not resting in God's peace in the times we live in because they do not spend enough time in God's presence. Financial pressure is one of the biggest things that keep us too busy to be available for God. Satan uses many weapons to attack an individual's mind in times of crisis, such as stress, anxiety, depression, discouragement about your calling, and the worst one is unbelief in the promises of God.

If this is your case, then consider this book as a divine appointment of God for your life that will renew your mind, bring about the healing of your faith, and help you believe that God has more for you because he is a God of second chances. The Bible says, "And we know that all things work together for good to them that love God, to those who are called according to his purpose." Rom. 8:28 (NIV)

God loves you so much that he wants to take all your failures and disappointments and use them to bless others, so what the enemy has meant for evil, God can turn it around and use it for good.

In general, if this book is in your hands, it means the God of all provision has closed so many doors to bring you to the right door, is preparing you to enter one of the best seasons of your life!

It is time for you to believe that you qualify for more.

You have experienced failure, and you may need to put in practice the prophetic words contained in this book to bring the necessary healing of your soul. You have forgotten that no matter how bad your present situation looks, God is still in control of everything in your life. The godly kingdom mentality that you used to have is long gone because you have prayed, fasted, and chased the Lord, and nothing changed, or you feel like you cannot continue to live the Christian life anymore, but I have good news for you! God has been working behind the scenes to prepare you to begin a better life, and the only thing you need to understand is that God works from the inside out and not backward.

The apostle Paul encourages us in the book of Romans Chapter 12 to renew our minds. As a teacher that moves in the prophetic word of knowledge, I am here to tell you that the worst is over for your life, and the best is yet to come!

I pray that you meditate in the message of this book, attend to the unity of the Holy Spirit of God so the power of the resurrection will restore the godly mentality that was stolen from you, through the cross by Jesus Christ.

I pray that this book will help you to receive the necessary healing of your faith so you will be able to press on to your destiny, even though times of difficulty. I pray that your mentality will renew the way God did it from your mother's womb.

Cordially,
Dr. Oscar Pelaez

PRAYER OF SALVATION

I AM GLAD THAT YOU MADE it to the end. If this material changed the way you think, spark the desire to be close to Jesus, or know more about Him, please, repeat this prayer, not with your mind but with your mouth. Because it says in the Bible, "For it is with your heart that you believe and are justified, and it is with your mouth that you profess your faith and are saved." Rom. 10:10 (NIV)

"Lord Jesus, forgive me for all my sins. Today, I call upon your name to come to my heart, and I receive you as my Lord and Savior. I declare that you came, die, and resurrect at the third day, rose to heavens, and He is at the right hand of the father in heavens. Thank you, Lord Jesus, for hearing my prayer. I declare that your blood washes me and cleanse me from all my sins, and set me free out of eternal condemnation, forgive me, forever. Amen and Amen!

Congratulations, you are now a son of the living God and have the Blessing of eternal life. God Bless!

ABOUT THE BOOK

IN GENERAL, IF THIS BOOK is in your hands, it means the God of all provision has closed so many doors to bring you the right door, preparing you to enter in one of the best seasons of your life! It is time for you to believe that you qualify for more.

You have experienced failure, and you may need to put in practice the prophetic words contained in this book to bring the necessary healing of your soul. You have forgotten that no matter how bad your present situation looks, God is still in control of everything in your life. The godly kingdom mentality that you used to have is long gone because you have prayed, fasted, and chased the Lord, and nothing changed, or you feel like you cannot continue to live the Christian life anymore, but I have good news for you! God has been working behind the scenes to prepare you to begin a better life, and the only thing you need to understand is that God works from the inside and not backward. The apostle Paul encourages us in Romans Chapter 12 to renew our minds. As a teacher that moves in the prophetic word of knowledge, I am here to tell you that the worst is over for your life, and the best is yet to come!

I pray that you meditate on the message of this book, attend to the unity of the Holy Spirit of God so the power of the resurrection will restore the godly mentality that was stolen from you, through the cross by Jesus Christ.

I pray that this book will help you to receive the necessary healing of your faith so you will be able to press on to your destiny, even through times of difficulty. I pray that your mentality will renew the way God did it from your mother's womb.